Introduction
Shoot Your Child's Show Like a Pro!

I0493755

HELP- THE SHOW IS TONIGHT!!!! I DON'T HAVE TIME TO READ THIS WHOLE BOOK!

If you just picked up this book because your child is in a show tonight and you are in a panic, this chapter is for you. Stop, take a deep breath, maybe have a quick adult beverage of your choice (assuming you aren't the one driving to the show) and read this chapter with your camera, the manual for your camera (if you have it) and your computer sitting right next to you. I will tell you how to set your camera up and how to take the pictures tonight, then you can come back later and read the rest of the book to learn the reasons why. For now you'll just have to trust me.

It should be obvious why you would want your camera and the manual next to you, but why the computer? Because I don't know what type of camera you have, therefore I cannot tell you how to find the settings I am describing on your particular brand and model. I use Nikon cameras and lenses- while I will try as much as possible to use generic terms for settings and features, the examples I give will be Nikon specific because that is what I am familiar with. I am assuming you have some sort of DSLR, in which case you should be able to control all the settings I am going to mention. Don't worry if you don't know what something means, that will be explained later in the book. Oh, and before you read any further make sure you have downloaded all the images on your memory card, then format the card in the camera so you'll have plenty of room. Once that is done put your battery on the charger so you'll have a full one (and hopefully a spare) when its' time to shoot, then read on.

Now, let's get down to business since there's no time to waste. Here's how to set up your camera.

Lens: If you only have one lens that came with your camera, it's probably an

18-55mm. If that's all you have, that's what you will use. If you have a longer zoom (probably something in the 100-300mm range) you should probably swap out and put that one on the camera. Bring both if you don't know how big the theater is or where you will be sitting. For most theaters if you have the 18-55mm you'd want to sit near the front, if you have a zoom that goes up to 200mm or 300mm you should be fine in the back row. Whichever you have, check it out when you get to the show and choose your seat accordingly. If you have room in your bag, bring both lenses and pick when you get there and see what you're dealing with.

Mode: Manual

Shutter Speed: 1/200 Sec

Aperture: F3.5 (or the smallest number / largest aperture your lens has available)

Flash: If you have an external flash, leave it off the camera. If you have a popup flash make sure it it down and stays down. (It shouldn't activate in shutter priority mode unless you pop it up manually, so don't)

ISO: Do a quick search on Google and find out what the highest useable ISO setting is for you particular camera and go with that, or if you want to be safe, one setting below that. If you can't find it quickly enough or don't even have time to look, use ISO 1600, that should be safe for any current generation DSLR. If you have a mirrorless system 1600 is probably also safe. Point and shoots aren't as capable at higher ISOs, so I really can't tell you what's safe for yours, you will have to look it up. NOTE- just because you camera has higher settings available doesn't mean they are useable in the sense I am talking about here. You may get a picture with them, but it will be so noisy you won't be happy with it. So don't just go to the highest setting you have.

Focus Mode: Continuous autofocus. If you have a choice of focus point numbers, pick the option that gives you a small cluster around the point of your choice. If you can set a focus delay, set it for normal or slightly longer. (This means if someone walks in front of your child right as you click the shutter the autofocus won't try to refocus on them instead of your child)

Metering Mode: Center weighted. The icon for this will probably look like a dot in between two parenthesis.

Noise Reduction: If your camera has a noise reduction option, turn it on and set it to normal.

Image Quality: If you have the option and a large enough memory card, set this to RAW + JPEG Fine, as this will give you the most options to work with later on. If you can't do both, either due to memory limitations or because your camera doesn't offer that option, stick with JPEG fine for now, especially if you want to share you pictures tonight or tomorrow. (If you are already shooting and working in RAW then by all means shoot RAW only)

Active Lighting: Turn it on and set it to the middle setting. (Active D for Nikon, Active Lighting Option for Canon, not sure for others)

Image Preview: Off. This means you won't see each image on your LCD screen after you shoot it. Trust me, this is a good thing.

Vibration Reduction / Image Stabilization: This one varies. If you have the standard 18-55mm lens, turn it off. If you have a longer zoom, leave it on. Generally, if your shutter speed is less than the focal length of the lens you want it on, if it's faster you want it off.

Shooting Mode: Single Shot

White Balance: If you use Auto your shots will not be consistent. Which setting to use will be dependent on the lights. If it's an outdoor show, use either the sun or cloudy setting. For indoors in a traditional theater, I recommend the tungsten setting if they use incandescent stage lights or the flash setting if they are using LED stage lights. If you don't know the difference, ask the lighting person if you can, if you can't find out which it is then use the tungsten setting.

Picture Controls: Standard or Neutral.

Exposure Meter: Not a setting, per se, but if you are not familiar with this display and how it shows up in your camera make sure you find it and have a basic understanding of how your camera displays Zero (what camera thinks is "proper" exposure), Overexposure (+) and Underexposure (-) values. If your camera lets you, set this to read in 1/3 stop increments. You manual should tell you what it looks like and where to find it on your camera display.

Ok, now your camera is set, let's talk about how to actually shoot the show.

Get to the theater as early as you can. You want to be walking into the theater as soon as they open the doors so you can get the best seat possible. Which seat this is depends on how big the theater is compared to what lens you have on your camera. If you have the basic 18-55mm you will want to be fairly close to the stage and near the center of the audience. (If you know your child will only be on one side of the stage and stay there, you want to be on that side of the audience). If you have a longer zoom you have more flexibility to sit farther back. Since I don't know what lens you have or the theater layout, I can't give you more specific advice. One thing I will recommend is (unless you get a front row center seat) if your theater has multiple audience sections, sit in one of the aisle seats on the inner edge of one of the outer sections of the audience, this will let you shoot most of the stage without being blocked by people in front of you or you blocking the view of people behind you.

If you are the official photographer (you hopefully know what you are doing and don't need to be reading this, but maybe you specialize in macro work and whoever asked you to shoot the show didn't realize that, or know what it meant, they just knew that a parent of one of the kids in the show was a photographer and asked you for help) then get in before the doors open and try to get the lighting team to show you a few cues so you can take test shots and adjust. If they have time to do this, try to get the darkest cue, the brightest cue and an average. Also ask them if there are any single color washes (these are the hardest to get right exposure wise).

If you aren't the official photographer, check and see if there are any restrictions on photography and if there are, respect them. If there aren't, and you will be shooting through the whole show, it may be better for you to find a place to stand on one of the side aisles so you won't be disturbing people seated next to you. If you are only shooting a small part of the show and/or stuck in your seat, just make sure you won't disturb your neighbors to much. Wherever you are shooting from, be aware that you won't be the only one trying to take pictures of their children performing. There may even be a professional hired to shoot the show. If someone is getting paid to shoot the show, please respect that and try to stay out of that person's way. Also, make sure you share the good angles with the other parents. Get your shot, then move so that they can get theirs. (if it makes you feel better, yours will be better than theirs because they haven't read this book - and when they ask, feel free to recommend my book, of course!)

You're in your seat, the lights are dimming and the curtain is opening. Time to get to work. Unless you know for sure exactly when your child will be onstage, turn your camera on and leave it on throughout the whole show. If your battery is fully charged you should have plenty of juice, especially since your auto preview and built in flash are both turned off. For musicals, dances or fast action scenes, set your shutter speed to at least 1/200 second to start out. If it's a regular play or a slower moving scene and your images look too dark, you can use a slower shutter speed, try 1/125 or 1/100 second. If your child is in the first scene, start shooting. If your child isn't in the first scene, shoot a few test frames at the beginning anyway. Focus on your child, or anyone in the light on the stage and press your shutter halfway so your camera focuses. When doing this, place your center focus point (which should also be your meter point unless you have set your camera otherwise) on what you want to be properly exposed. Normally this will be your subject's face. Just be aware that if the costume is significantly brighter or darker than your subject's face you may have to use that as a target instead to get the result you want.

While keeping the shutter pressed halfway take a look at the exposure meter bar in your viewfinder. If it reads Zero or pretty close to zero (within about three bars/dots) you are probably good with your settings. If the exposure meter reads significantly off one way or the other you may have to make adjustments. The easiest way to adjust is to change your shutter speed. While keeping the shutter button pressed halfway, rotate your main dial (if you are set up as I described this will adjust shutter speed). If your meter is too high (more than three bars on the plus side) increase your shutter speed (i.e. 1/320, 1/500. Etc) until you are within three bars of zero. If it reads too low, use a slower shutter speed if you can. The reason I say "if you can" is that if you get below 1/200 sec for dance or fast moving scenes, or 1/100 sec for regular scenes, it becomes very likely that you will get blurry images because your subjects are moving. You will have to take a few quick test shots at the shutter speed you need and if there is too much motion blur you will need to increase your ISO to so you can shoot at faster shutter speeds. It is very unlikely that there will be so much light that you can't adjust shutter speed high enough to get your exposure into the right range, but if you find that you need to go up to 1/1000 sec or above to get in the zone, consider yourself lucky and lower your ISO by a notch or two. One caveat you should look out for is single color wash lighting - in other words the entire stage is lit with a single color light. Red is the worst case, green is the best, but in general because of the way camera sensors are designed this is a difficult situation for them to get a correct reading, so you want to underexpose from what your camera meter reads by at least 2-3 bars (one stop). This means raise your shutter speed until you are 2-3 bars into the (-) reading on your meter.

Once you have your meter reading within three bars of zero, take a test shot or two and look at the results in your LCD screen. If the images are too dark overall you need to use a slower shutter speed or higher ISO. If they are too bright overall then you need a faster shutter speed or a lower ISO. If parts of your image are in crisp focus but things like hands/legs/hair are blurry you probably have motion blur and need a faster shutter speed. If nothing is in sharp focus (your camera probably wouldn't have let you take the picture as this is how most are set by default) then your auto focus system is having trouble. This may happen because it is simply too dark or because there is not enough contrast (i.e. You are trying to focus on a dark costume against a solid black stage curtain, or the reverse) Make any adjustments you need, take a couple more test shots and see if you got the result you wanted. Once you have things pretty much dialed in where you like them, turn the LCD screen back off and don't look at it again unless the lighting or the action changes significantly and you need to readjust. Watch the exposure meter as you shoot and adjust your shutter speed on the fly to keep it close to zero. You do not want to be looking at the LCD screed after each shot. This practice is referred to as "chimping" in photographic lingo. Not only does it disturb your neighbors and distract them from the show, but you also are likely to miss great shots while you are checking to see if you got the last one. You either did or didn't. While we are discussing looking at the preview images on your camera's LCD screen, let me give you one additional tidbit of advice. Unless you are low on memory and need to clear space, never delete images based on what you see on the camera. Always wait until you get the images onto your computer. Not only is the image on that preview screen not always a good representation of what your actual image will look like, but deleting on the camera also increases the chance of card errors problems with other images.

On the subject of missing things, the ideal time to click the shutter is the millisecond before the shot happens. Each camera will have its' own distinct shutter lag- the time it takes between you pressing the button and the camera firing. This isn't a setting, it's just a factor inherent to camera design- generally speaking the higher end cameras in each type will have less shutter lag and DSLRs will generally have less lag than their point and shoot counter parts. You need to be familiar with yours so you can click at the appropriate instant. The irony of shooting with a DSLR is that you will not see your picture through the viewfinder, you will see what happened right before your picture and what happened right after. That means that if you see something in your viewfinder, it's to late, you missed the shot. There are two ways to minimize this: first, while your child is performing, keep your focus point on them and the shutter button half pressed. If your camera is set up properly your autofocus should follow them and keep them in focus so you are ready to shoot. The second technique is a bit more advanced, although some people pick it up more easily than others- two eyed shooting. You keep one eye on the viewfinder and what is going on with the camera and the other on the real world so you can see more of the big picture. If you have never done this before I don't recommend trying it for the first time today unless you want to practice a few frames shooting while your child isn't on stage. It takes some getting used to for most of us.

On a related note- since you cannot see what is happening while your camera is taking the picture, and you are going to want to take pictures at all the big moments in your child's performance, you will actually miss most of your child's performance. Don't get so caught up in taking pictures that you don't actually experience and enjoy the show. Every now and then I go to a show and leave my camera at home. Even though I twitch a little bit when I see images I wish I could have captured, it's worth it to actually see the show for a change.

Once the show is over and you have taken your child out for post show ice cream and are back home, I recommend you do a few things as soon as possible. First, transfer your images onto your computer. Once they are uploaded, before you even look at them, run whatever software you use for a backup so you now have three copies of your images, including the card you shot them on. While this is happening, charge your batteries and reset your camera to the settings you normally use so it will be ready when you next need it. If you shot RAW plus JPEG and aren't used to working with RAW files yet, put the JPEG images (the ones with .JPEG or .JPG after the filename) where you usually put your images and treat them like you do your other pictures. Put the RAW images (the other ones) in a separate folder to come back to later, if you want to once you have read further. Once you have your images on your computer and backed up at least once (most pros have multiple backup systems) then you can format your card and be ready for the next shoot.

After your images are on the computer and backed up, it's finally time to go grab a glass of wine, sit down and look through them. If you've followed the steps above you should have gotten a lot of keepers. That being said, don't be discouraged if there are more misses than hits, my first show I shot about 1200 frames and wound up with around 200 shots worth putting online. A few years and lots of performances later, I am taking a lot less frames per show and have a much higher keeper ratio. If you stick with it your hit rate will go up as well.

Now that the emergency is over, you can take some time and read on. I will explain why I had you set things up the way I did and shoot the way you did, and give you some tips and techniques to use on the images you took to make them even better.

Ok, Now that you're either past your crisis night or just coming in fresh, let's get started.

Who This Book Is For

If you are a photojournalist or a professional photographer who shoots live events for a living, you aren't going to learn much from this book. If you are a professional photographer who shoots some other type of photography for a living: commercial, fashion, landscapes, etc, you will hopefully find some useful information for making the transition to shooting live performances, but you will also be bored to tears while I go over the basics and you can safely skip the bulk of the book.

This book is designed for the parent who has a DSLR camera that they have been using mostly in the Program (P) mode to record family vacations, holidays and birthdays and is getting ready to try and shoot their child's first performance and wants to know what to do. Or maybe someone who has tried to photograph a performance or two and been disappointed with their results. If these descriptions are close to the mark then this book is for you. Hopefully by the time we're done you will feel comfortable taking your camera out of the program mode and confidently using some of those dials, buttons, menus and settings that seem so unfathomable right now.

How To Get The Most Out of This Book

If you are just picking this up and the show is tonight, go back to the Emergency Section at the beginning. If not read on. In order to use this book you will at least need your camera and its' instruction manual in front of you and it will also be helpful to be near a computer with an internet connection so you can access the all powerful oracle of the web. I will explain what you need to do to set up and use your camera and why I am making each particular recommendation, but you will be on your own when it comes to the "how" for your particular camera. There are simply too many different camera brands and models out there for me to attempt to tell each of you how to activate or change each setting on yours. I will be using the most standard, common names for settings and functions I can, but what I refer to as one thing may be called something different on your camera. While I will try to be as generic as possible, I will default to Nikon terms and labels because that is what I use on a daily basis and am most familiar with. If you can't find something on your particular camera or in the manual, a quick search on the web for "how to set xxx on (your camera make/model)" should get you the specific instructions you need. If you have a point and shoot, you may not have access to some or any of the functions or settings I refer to here, but any DSLR or mirrorless camera should have some variation of all of the basic settings and functions.

Who I Am

Let's start with me; who I am and what makes me think I am qualified to give you photography advice. I was born and raised in New Orleans, Louisiana. I lived there from birth to age eighteen. (That has nothing to do with photography, but you have to start a bio somewhere, right?) I got my first "serious" camera, a Canon AE1-P, in 1989 as a Christmas present from my parents. Before that I had been taking snapshots with a 110mm point and shoot. I enjoyed taking pictures and seeing them come back from the developer to see what I had gotten. This was in the dark ages before digital cameras, when you actually had no idea what you had captured and couldn't find out until you got your film developed and got it back unless you had a Polaroid. I decided being a photographer was fun and asked for a 35mm camera setup for Christmas. Santa must have been listening (i.e. My ever supportive parents scrimped and saved all year) and got me that Canon. I think I had a 50mm prime and an 80-200mm zoom lens that came with the kit. I started shooting as much as film as I could afford to get developed. My high school had a darkroom so I even learned how to do my own black and white developing and printing. I loved being able to see the images come to life on the paper. Sadly, my house got robbed and I lost that camera setup. I wasn't able to replace it until college when I was able to save up enough to get another SLR, this time a Nikon 6006. Just as I was getting back into shooting with something better than a point and shoot, my apartment got robbed and I lost that camera as well. I was young, dumb and poor and since I hadn't heard of renter's insurance I was pretty much out of luck. Serious photography fell by the wayside for me for several years until I had the time, resources and motivation to revisit my passion for photography.

While I was in high school learning to work with that first SLR I also found a passion for theater, both on stage and as a technician and lighting designer. I enjoyed this enough that I wound up not only working in with several professional theaters in town, but also attending an intensive three year theater arts program at the New Orleans Center for Creative Arts. When I wasn't on stage or in the lighting booth I was shooting the shows. I would have included some of those old shots with this book, but sadly they were in my parents house in New Orleans and didn't survive the flooding after Hurricane Katrina.

After high school I joined the Navy because I wanted the government to pay for college. Thanks to the Navy I wound up in Southern California where I discovered circus arts and became a circus performer as well as instructor. When I picked up serious photography again I decided to combine the two passions and have spent the past couple of years shooting circus performers, burlesque shows, fire dancers and theater and dance festivals in addition to some large arena concerts. I have shot shows outdoors under bright noonday sun and in the darkest poorly lit nightclubs. I have found many techniques that work and many more that do not. I am by no means the foremost expert on stage photography out there, but I have learned a lot and I think I can give you enough information from my experience to allow you to take fabulous pictures of your children's performances that you will be able to enjoy and share with others.

Most of the the shows I shoot are circus or dance, and most of the performers are adults, so most of the images in this book reflect that, but the techniques I use will work just as well at your child's dance recital or Shakespeare festival. All the images in the book are shots I have taken and edited myself, starting with the cover- my son may not be old enough to play Hamlet yet, but he does a passable Peter Pan, right?

The Basics

Now let's cover some basics.

Cameras

Since this is a photography book, the first thing to discuss is cameras. This book is focused primarily on the DSLR, or Digital Single Lens Reflex camera, which is the follow on to the 35mm film SLR. If you are shooting with another style of camera, you will still be able to find some useful information in this book, but you will have to adapt it a bit to make it fit your particular tool. Other common camera types out there are the Point and Shoots (which do not have interchangeable lenses in most cases), mirrorless cameras and the ubiquitous cellphone camera. Less common but still out there in use are film SLRs, and Medium/Large Format cameras (larger than 35mm film/sensor) for both film and digital. If you are shooting with a Medium or Large format camera, this book is probably written way below your level, sorry. For the rest of you, I will discuss sensor sizes in greater detail later.

If you already own a DSLR or mirrorless system you are in good shape. As long as it is a fairly recent model you have the capability to produce great images with the gear you have. If all you have is a point and shoot, it may have the features you need to shoot your child's shows, but you will get better results from a DSLR. I'll discuss the differences between entry level, prosumer and professional level DSLRs later, but for now I will just say that any recent model entry level DSLR and kit lens (kit lens just means the lens that came with the camera "kit" you bought) should be able to produce good, useable images under the average conditions you are likely to find at your children's performances. If you are looking at upgrading from a point and shoot, relax, you don't have to buy the top of the line high end cadillac model.

One of the most frequent questions in any beginning photography discussion is some variation on "which camera is best," or "which camera should I buy?" If I could give a definitive answer for you I would, but there isn't one. Any entry level DSLR from one of the major names will be more than sufficient for shooting your family in most situations, including performances, so how do you choose? First, if you are starting from zero and have no idea what you want, read this book, at least the first couple of sections on definitions and settings. Reading these will give you a basic framework to evaluate the statistics and capabilities of the camera choices out there. Second, you need to figure out your price range, then look around online and see what your options are given your budget. Once you have narrowed the selection down, go online to sites like DPreview.com and see what the reviewers say about the various makes and models you can afford. Finally, when you have narrowed your selection down to a few models that have the capabilities you need and fit your budget, head to a local camera shop and actually try each one out. Hold each one, look through the viewfinder, play with the controls and menus and, if you can, just shoot a few frames. Within any given price range the various models will all be fairly close to each other capability wise, so the choice will ultimately come down to which one feels best in your hand and which control layout and menu setup is most intuitive and easiest for you to learn and use. If plan on sticking with photography for a while and possibly getting more serious down the line, make sure you look at expandability- what systems of lenses, flashes and other toys you will be able to use with your camera later on. I recommend sticking with one of the major brands for this reason, it will give you more room to grow later on without having to learn a whole new system.

Lenses

Most entry and prosumer level DSLRs will come packaged with a "kit" lens or possibly two. The most common kit lens will be something in the 18-55mm F3.5-F5.6 range. If there is a second lens it will be something with a bit more reach but a similar aperture range. You can also buy just a camera body with no lens included. This is more common in the higher end bodies because people buying these may already have a range of lenses to choose from, or would rather pick the specific lenses they need for their own style of photography. Again, these kit lenses will all be sufficient for shooting snapshots of your family, vacation pictures and almost any performance scenario. I will discuss the specific benefits and of higher end "pro" lenses later on in this book, but their main limitations initially are that they are far more expensive to purchase and will generally be larger and heavier than their consumer level counterparts. Another factor in lens choice is that you are not necessarily limited to the same manufacturer as your camera body. There are several "third party" lens companies that make lenses to fit cameras from the major brands. These lenses will generally be less expensive than a similar level lens from the manufacturer and can be close, if not equal (or even better in some cases) in capability. Sigma and Tamron are probably the two biggest names in this market, although there are others.

In general, there are two categories of lenses- Primes and Zooms. Prime lenses only have one focal length, this means that the only way to zoom in or out is to physically move closer to or farther away from your subject. This is known as "zooming with your feet." Zoom lenses have a range of focal lengths that you can select by rotating a ring or pushing/pulling the lens body, which changes the relationships of the glass inside the lens, thus the magnification of your subject. In general primes are simpler and relatively less expensive, and usually are able to let in more light for a given focal length that zooms because they have a smaller number of elements the light must pass through. Zooms offer more flexibility but generally cost more and cannot open up as wide as primes for light transmission. An important distinction is that these lenses offer OPTICAL zoom. Cell phone cameras and lower end point and shoots will frequently offer DIGITAL zoom, which is very different. In digital zoom, there is no physical change in the lens or in the recorded light, all digital zoom means is that the image will be cropped in camera, with a corresponding loss of resolution. A 12mp camera with digital zoom may only give you a 2mp image or worse using digital zoom, but with optical zoom you get a magnified image that still retains the full resolution of your sensor.

If you have a little more room in your budget when you are outfitting yourself initially, it is a far better investment to spend your money on upgrading your lenses rather than your camera body. As long as the camera body you purchase meets your minimum requirements, you will generally get much more improvement in your shooting capability from a lens upgrade than a body upgrade. (I say more capability- this is a fine but important point- better gear will give you more shooting options, but better gear will NOT automatically improve your photographic ability nor will it magically make your pictures better. In fact, as I will discuss in the pro gear section, it may actually initially make your images worse). Lenses also hold their value much better than camera bodies. With some exceptions, a 20 year old camera body is probably worthless to anyone except a collector, while many 20 year old lenses are still just as useful today as they were the day they were made, and some even sell for more than their original price. Depending on your camera system, you may still be able to use those older lenses with your new digital camera bodies. This is one of the advantages of the Nikon system. I can grab a 20 year old lens and slap it onto my D4 and it will work just as well as it would on an older Nikon F body. Not all manufacturers offer backwards compatibility like that.

What I use

I started out the digital iteration of my photographic journey with a Nikon D3200 and the included 18-55mm F3.6-5.6 Kit lens. At the time, this was the lowest end of the Nikon DSLR range. Some of the images in this book were shot with that combination. Once I had used this setup for a while and realized I was going to be shooting a lot more performances in poorly lit theaters, I upgraded to a couple of professional lenses. Finally, when I decided to try and set myself up to transition into photography as a career I decided to upgrade to a professional body as well. Now I shoot shows with a D4 and a range of fast zooms. I also keep a fast prime in the bag for the very dark nightclub shows.

My Recommendations

You will be able to get great shots using an entry level DSLR and kit lens. If you already have a DSLR, relax, you will be able to use what you have. You do not need to rush out and buy the latest, greatest, top of the line gear. If you don't already have a camera, read the book, learn what you need, then decide what to buy based on what you can afford and what works best in your hand. But, you didn't buy this book just to get generalities so if you want my opinion- I think the best camera setup (for low light action shooting) on the market at the time of this writing is the Nikon D4S (I don't have one yet, but if enough of you buy this book I may just get one) accompanied by the Nikon 24-70mm f2.8 and 70-200mm F2.8 VRII lenses. If you have an unlimited budget and absolutely have to buy the best right now, that's the way to go. If Canon cameras fit your hand better, I believe the 5DMKIII and equivalent lens setup is their best contender, but I prefer the Nikon ergonomics. Of course, by the time you read this there may have been a new development. The camera business is an arms race, each time one of the major competitors puts out something newer, faster and better, the others follow suit and try to go one up again. Camera capabilities seem to always be on the increase, and some say mirrorless cameras are going to make DSLRs obsolete in the near future. This may or may not be true, but for now at the top end of the performance scale, DSLRs are still winning. So do your research, buy only what you need and can afford, if there is a chance you will stick with photography, make sure you are buying into a system that gives you room to expand, and invest in better lenses before better cameras. Just remember, better gear WILL NOT automatically make your pictures better, and even though the combo I just recommended would set you back close to $10k, you will be able to get great shots of your children's shows from just about any entry level DSLR kit you choose if you use it correctly, so you do not need to break the bank.

Critical Background Information

Let's Get Technical

Before we get into how to set your camera up and why, we need to go over some important terms and concepts. You don't need to become an expert in any of these right away and I will only scratch the surface of these topics, but a general level of knowledge will help you out in understanding the rest of this book. As you continue in your photographic journey you may find you want to learn more. I will add some links at the very end for further study if you are so inclined.

How your camera sees

Although the mechanics may vary, all types of cameras essentially function the same way. Lenses focus light onto a sensor, whether that sensor is film or digital. A digital sensor is made up of an array of individual receptor sites, and a single receptor site is called a pixel. A frame of film is similar but the sites are chemical rather than electronic. The resolution of your camera is a function of the number of receptor sites your sensor has, hence the xx Megapixel (mega = a million) designator on your camera. (And as we'll see shortly, just having more megapixels doesn't make one sensor better than another, so don't think a 41mp phone camera is better than a 16mp professional DSLR)

Each pixel can only see one color, and they are divided between the three primary colors of light: Red, Green and Blue (RBG). Green is the most dominant color in the human visible spectrum, so camera sensors are weighted towards the green end of the spectrum. There is some variation between cameras but usually the ratio will be roughly 60% green pixels, 20% red and 20% blue. Normally this isn't an issue, but under stage lighting it can cause some problems, which I will discuss later on.

How good your sensor is in low light is a function of several variables. In general, the newer your camera- therefore the newer your sensor- the more sensitive it will be to light and therefore better in low light conditions. The larger the individual sensor site is, the more receptive to light it will be, and the less densely packed the sites are the more accessible they will be to light. This means that for a set number of pixels a larger sensor will spread them out wider and it will be a better low light performer. Similarly, if the sensor size stays constant, the lower the pixel count, the wider the spacing and the better the low light performance. This is one of the main reasons why your 41mp phone camera with a relatively small sensor will not perform as well in low light as a 16mp DSLR with a larger sensor. I will discuss the different DSLR sensor sizes later but they are generally larger than those used in point and shoot cameras. I have to be careful and say "generally," because camera makers are always innovating and there is at least one full frame point and shoot on the market right now.

Light gets to the sensor via your lens. I will not go into optics in detail, if you are curious as to the physics of lenses there are many places you can find and learn to your level of scientific interest. For our purposes, you just need to understand that different types and designs of lenses gather the light differently, thus you can have different levels of magnification and different levels of ability to transmit light through the lens.

Once light goes through the lens and hits the sensor, the data from each pixel is stored on your memory card and your image is recorded for later viewing. On DSLR cameras, until you trip the shutter there is a mirror between your lens and the sensor. This mirror reflects the view from your lens up through another series of mirrors to the optical viewfinder on the rear of your camera. In point and shoot or mirrorless cameras, whether you are using the screen on the back of the camera or the electronic viewfinder (which is just a secondary miniature screen) you are seeing a digital representation vice the actual light through your lens. DSLRs also have electronic view screens you can use in addition to the optical viewfinder. If you want to see what I am talking about, take off your lens and look into the opening, there will be a mirror there. If you want (and your camera lets you- some don't) you can turn it on and fire the shutter with the lens off and you can see the mirror move out of the way to expose the sensor. This is why you will not be able to see what your sensor sees at the moment of capture and the viewfinder will be blank for the instant you are taking the picture.

Now that you know the basics of how your camera sees, let's go over some other background information and terms. You don't need to become an expert in theses things unless you really want to, but understanding what they are will enable me to explain why I am making the recommendations I am when I tell you how to set up your camera and also help you understand the differences between various camera and lens choices when you go shopping.

White Balance

Not all light is created equal. You may have noticed this if you have shopped for light bulbs recently, there are a plethora of "daylight balanced" bulbs out there designed to recreate sunlight more accurately than traditional bulbs. Your eyes and brain are a really magical system that compensates for different qualities of light so well that you almost never notice it, but different types of light are actually shifted towards different colors. You only get to notice this with your eyes in very extreme cases, like the heavy orange tint to the light from those high pressure sodium vapor street lights. It is more subtle in most cases and your eyes compensate for it without your conscious awareness, even if it does cause some unconscious mood shifts. (Do a quick search for light therapy to see what I am talking about) This slight shift in color of light is referred to in a couple of terms. It is measured numerically as Color Temperature (using a Kelvin scale) but is referred to in camera terminology as White Balance. Here's a quick explanation of both terms and how they effects your shots.

If you really want to get all scientific and technical, color temperature of light is based on the wavelength (therefore color) of light that would be radiated by a theoretical object called a "black body" at a given temperature. I am not going to go into more technical detail than that because it may make both our brains hurt. Higher color temperatures are closer to the white/blue end of the spectrum, while lower temperatures are in the red/orange end of the spectrum. The way to remember this is to think of a campfire versus the bunsen burner you may have had in your high school science lab, maybe there is still one in your young superstar's school right now. The red/orange campfire burns with a much cooler flame than the blue/white bunsen burner torch. So, higher color temperature means there is a more blueish white tint to the light. I know it's hard to think of one fire being cooler than another, but trust me, it's true.

25

This is where it really gets confusing. Let me re-state that higher "color temperature" numbers mean bluer light and lower numbers mean redder light. However, we are used to thinking of reds and oranges as "warm" and blue and white as "cold" colors. This time think campfire versus an iceberg. This terminology takes a while to get your head around, but it means that when we talk about "warmer" light we are actually talking about lower color temperatures and when we talk about "cooler" light we are talking about higher color temperatures. So it's a bit backwards. Luckily you don't really have to fully wrap your head around that dichotomy to figure out the white balance setting on your camera.

White Balance is your camera's way to adjust what the sensor records to compensate for the different light temperatures that may be present in the shot. Your eyes can automatically adjust for different color temperatures, your camera can't. (Ok- full disclosure, if your camera has an automatic white balance setting - and almost all DSLRs do- they can adjust automatically, but your eyes can adjust for multiple color temperature light sources at the same time and in the same image, but your camera really can only adjust to one at a time) Time for another experiment. Find out how to manually set the white balance for your camera. Most will give you several preset options for different common light sources, Tungsten, flash, sun, cloudy (diffused sunlight) and fluorescent are the most common. Tungsten is a fancy name for the old style of common lightbulbs, you may also see this setting / type of light referred to as incandescent, these bulbs use a tungsten filament to generate light. Most cameras will also give you the option of setting a custom white balance or dialing in a specific color temperature. (These last two options are well outside the scope of what you need for this book, so we'll stick to the presets for our purposes) Once you know how to set your white balance manually, find a partner, preferably one wearing a white shirt, have them stand somewhere you can stay for a minute or two. Pick a white balance setting on your camera, and take a picture. Change the white balance and take another picture. Repeat until you have gone through all your white balance presets. Look through the series of images on your camera and see if you can spot the difference. If not, here's a couple of examples. This is the same shot, the only difference between the three is the white balance setting.

First using the "flash" white balance setting.

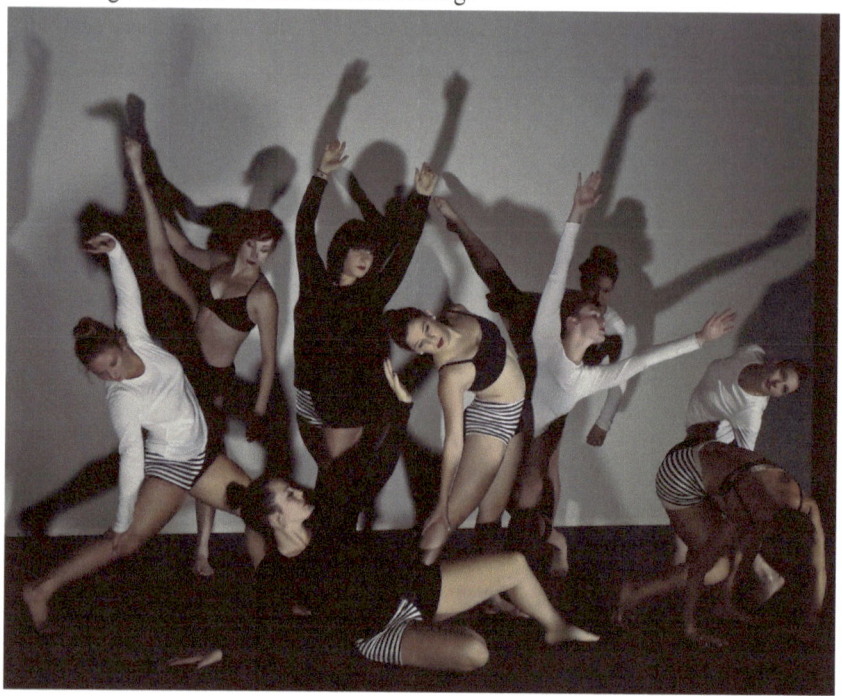

Next using the Sun/Daylight setting. Note there isn't much difference here, flash is pretty close to mid day sun in terms of temperature/white balance.

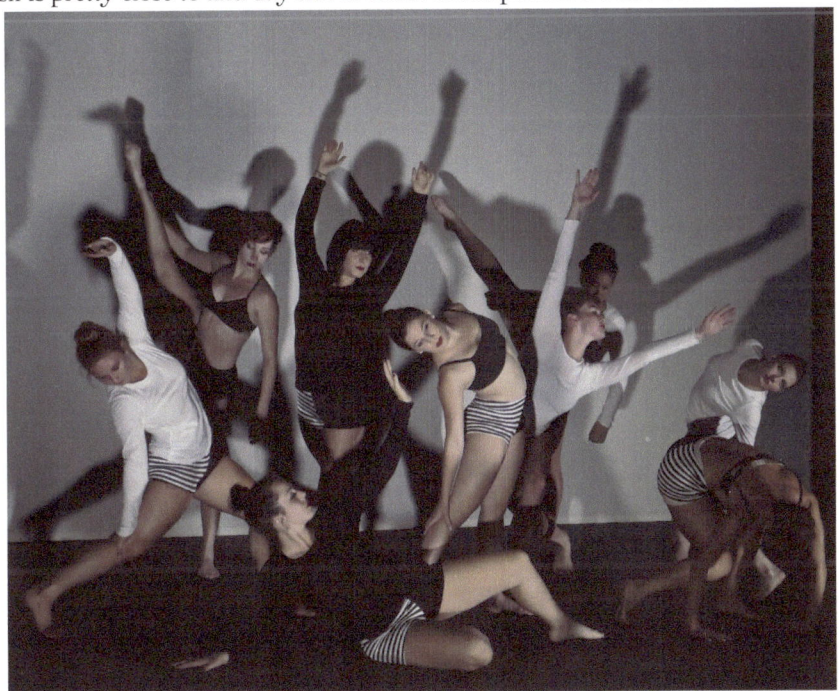

Finally let's switch the WB to Tungsten... tungsten, or incandescent light, is usually warmer, so the correction would be to cool the image down, hence the blue tones that appear in this version.

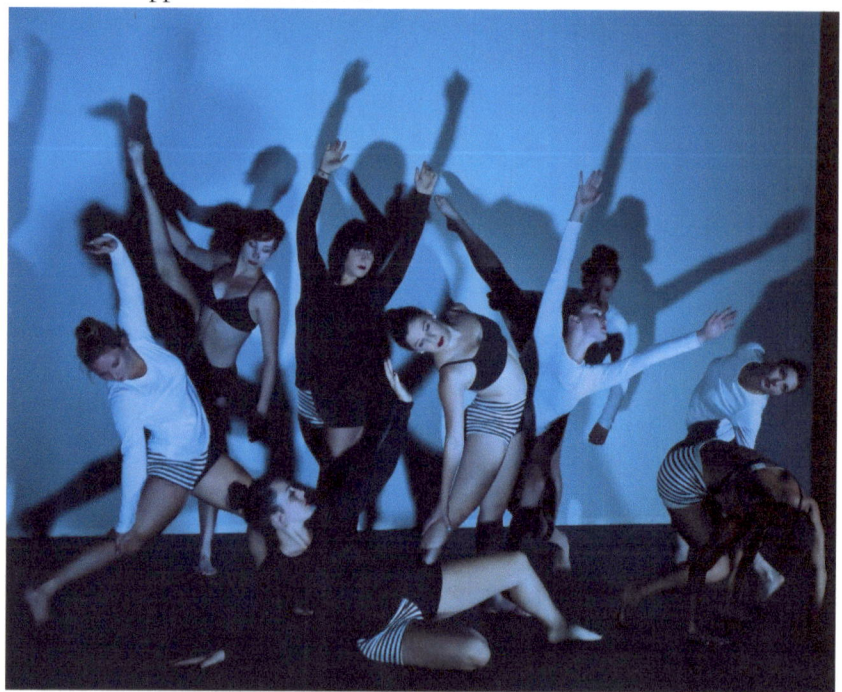

The reason this setting is called "white balance" in a camera is that what you are tying to do with this setting is tell the camera's brain how to compensate for the color temperature of the predominant light source of the scene in a way that something that is supposed to be white, and appears white to your eye (which automatically compensates) will appear white in your recorded image. (Actually the camera is balancing for 14-18% grey depending on your particular camera, but that's a technicality and has the same effect, again - more detail than we need to go in to here) To see what I mean, go back and look at the white shirts on the dancers in the sample images, and the background wall.

In general, tungsten is warmer/redder, flash is cooler/bluer, fluorescent lights are cool and greenish, and sunlight varies with time of day and how cloudy it is. You don't really have to understand white balance in detail for shooting performances, but I would have been remiss if I didn't mention it as it as important for most areas of photography. Also, if you look back at your shots and the colors don't seem to match what you remembered seeing, White Balance is the most likely reason for this, and changing it in post is probably the way to get back to what you saw. If you've ever taken a shot with a flash and your subject looked like a ghost while people in the background not lit by the flash looked normal, it's because the light temperatures, therefore the white balances, were different and your camera could only capture one properly at a time. We'll talk about how to set WB for your child's show later so that if your star looks like a green monster, it will be because of their makeup or the lighting, not your camera work.

Exposure Value (aka Stops of light)

Back in the film days, to take a picture you exposed your film to the light and it was recorded. These days, you expose your digital sensor. The measurement of the amount of light reaching your sensor for any given image is called your Exposure Value (EV) and is measured in units called Stops. Just for reference, the human eye can deal with a tremendous range of light compared to a camera. Your eyes can automatically compensate for somewhere around 13 stops worth of light without you having to think about it. The best DSLRs out there only have a range of about 3 or 4 stops for any given image. (This range is known in camera terms as Dynamic Range) This is part of why lots of times your pictures simply cannot live up to what you actually saw when you were shooting. Digital cameras are amazing and constantly improving, but the more I use them and understand their limitations, the more amazed I am by the tremendous capabilities of the human eye. (If you are familiar with HDR photography, this technique is a way to artificially extend the range of the camera, but it isn't a practical technique for shooting performances because it doesn't work well with moving subjects as the main focal point)

Each full Stop, or 1 EV, worth of change in the amount of light reaching your sensor represents either doubling, or halving of the total amount of light being recorded. A properly exposed, or neutral, image would have an EV of 0 on your camera's internal scale. Increasing your exposure by a full stop (+1EV) would mean that double the light reaches your sensor compared to the neutral exposure, thus the image would appear brighter. On the other side, decreasing your exposure by a full stop (-1EV) would mean half the light of the neutral image and thus would appear darker. We will discuss camera controls in detail later but the two major camera controls that effect amount of light reaching your sensor are Shutter Speed and Aperture. There are two other settings that also effect the exposure, ISO and Exposure Compensation, but these effect the sensor itself to change how the exposure is recorded but don't change the actual amount of light reaching the sensor.

Whether you use your camera's optical viewfinder or the electronic screen, you will be able to see a display of Exposure Value. Different manufacturers represent this differently but it will always be some sort of bar graph. It may be vertical on one side or the other or your viewfinder, or horizontal on the bottom (I have not seen one on the top, but I haven't looked through every viewfinder out there.) Regardless of where it appears, it will be a bar graph, with a 0 value in the center and a set of bars or dots going off to either side of zero. It may appear in your viewfinder as well as on an external screen if your camera has one. It generally will be visible as well on your LCD if you use the Live View mode. There are a variety of options for how your camera can display exposure value information on this graph, you will have to consult your manual to see how yours provides you information, and you may even be able to customize the display to fit your personal preferences. Most cameras allow you to display exposure value in either Full, 1/2 or 1/3 stop increments. You may also be able to select which direction on your graph represents a positive or negative change in EV. (If you can change this setting, and it isn't set so by default, I recommend you set it so that the change in EV on the scale mirrors the way you rotate your main control dial in your most common shooting mode: Say you shoot mostly in manual mode, so your primary dial will be shutter speed. If rotate your dial right with your thumb to increase shutter speed, therefore decrease exposure, you would want the negative exposure side of your graph on the right in the viewfinder)

While trying to come up with an image for this section, I discovered that it is really, really difficult to get a good image of what you see looking through your viewfinder, so I decided to try and make a graphic for you. Your manual should have a much better representation of your exposure indicator and where to find it, but if it helps, whether you are looking through your viewfinder, on your camera's information display panel, or using live view, you are looking for something that looks roughly like this:

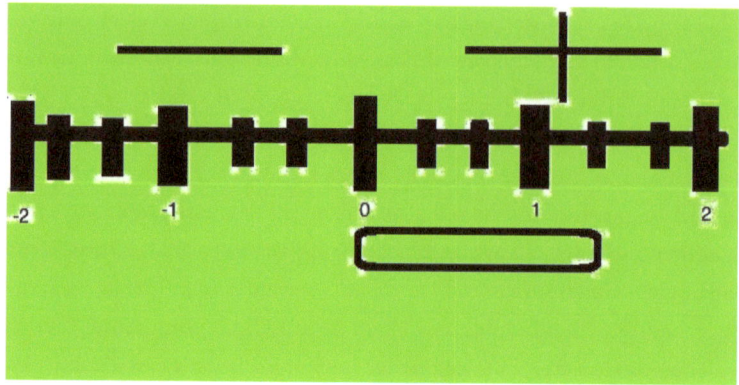

NOTE: On Nikon cameras, the exposure indicator will only be visible in manual mode or when you have some amount of exposure compensation dialed in. With no exposure compensation, you will only see the meter while in any automatic mode if the exposure is so far outside the range that the camera cannot get it close to zero with the automatic settings available. Other camera makers may differ but likely will function in a similar manner.

I will discuss in more detail how to use this meter while shooting, but for now just to familiarize yourself with it, turn your camera on, set it to manual mode (M), (make sure you don't have ISO set to auto) point it at at anything nearby and reasonably well lit, like a white wall, and look through the viewfinder. Press the shutter button half way and you should see your meter become visible. For this exercise it doesn't matter what it initially reads, you aren't trying to take a great picture. You should have a knob right near your right thumb that controls shutter speed in manual mode. While keeping your eye on the viewfinder and the shutter button half pressed, rotate this knob one direction and watch your meter bar. For each click in one direction you should see a corresponding change of one dot/bar on your exposure meter. Turn the control knob until your meter bar shows halfway or more to one side, and take a picture. Turn your dial the opposite direction until the exposure bar reads 0, or is in the center, and take another picture. Finally, continue past 0 the opposite direction until your meter reads as far to the opposite side of the graph as it did for your first shot and take a third picture. Stop and look at the three pictures. Although the order may vary depending on where you started, you should have one image that is too bright (overexposed), one that is properly exposed (the center of the meter) and a third that is too dark (underexposed). Play with this a bit and once you get used to it you will get a feel for how those little bars on your screen translate into how your images will look.

Here is an example for you; just like with White Balance, this is the same image with the exposure altered afterwards so you can see the difference.

The correct, or 0 exposure

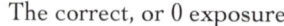

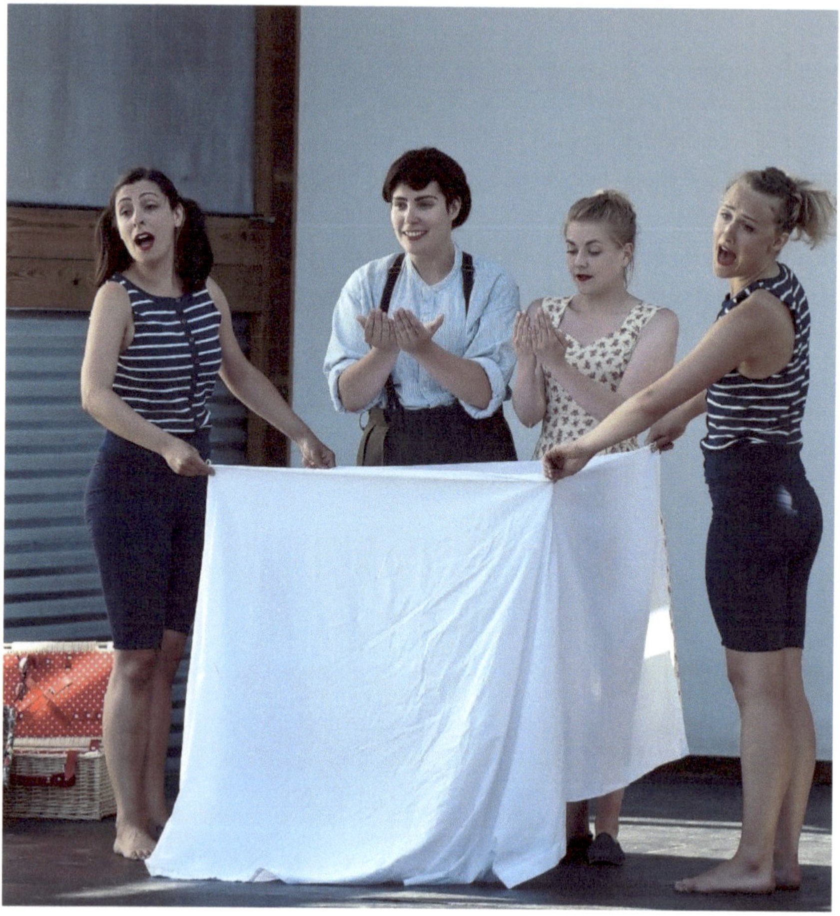

Underexposed by three stops (-3ev)

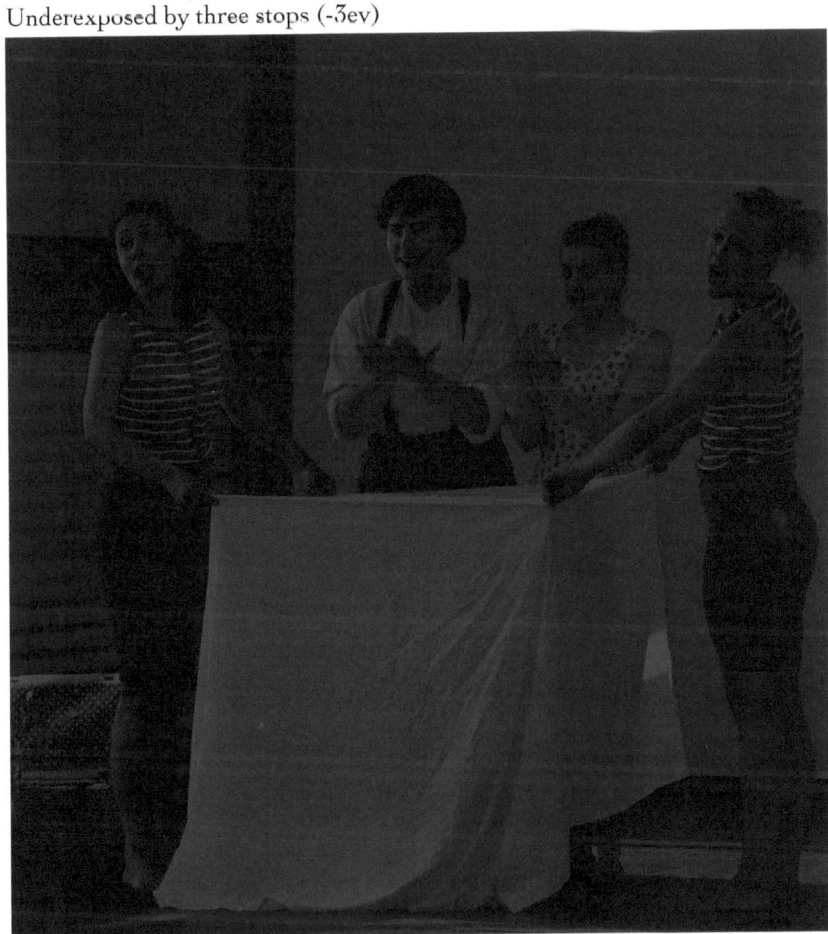

Overexposed by three stops (+3ev)

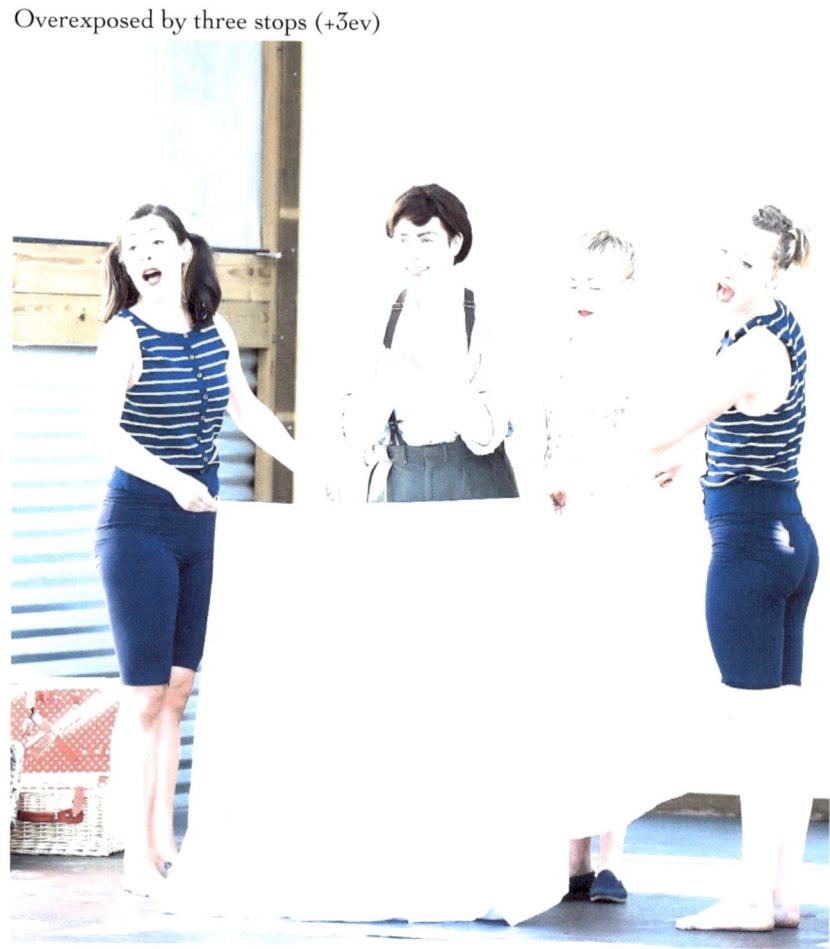

Metering and Exposure Compensation

Your camera has a built in light meter. You can also purchase an external light meter, although these aren't really going to be useful for you in the standard performance setting, so I won't discuss them here. While we will be talking about shooting mostly in manual mode, even if you shoot in your camera's program or auto modes, it is still useful for you to understand how these meters work and how yours is set. When you activate your camera's meter by pressing the shutter halfway down, it looks at the light coming in through your lens and compares what it sees against an internal database. From this database it tries to find the closest overall match to what it sees and returns the corresponding recommended exposure value for that closest match. These meters are calibrated to try and reduce the brightest highlights to an overall neutral grey and make an average image from the input it receives. You can modify how the camera weights the different amounts of light in the scene by how you set your meter. Also, please note that when I say, "what the camera sees," I am talking about levels and percentages of the various colors of light. The camera has no idea if that light is coming from a landscape scene or a prima ballerina on stage at the Met.

Although different manufacturers will use slightly different terminology, your camera probably has three distinct metering modes. One will take into account the lighting in the whole frame with approximately equal weight. One will use a relatively large area around the center of the frame. The third will only use a very small point at the center of your frame. (Some cameras will let you adjust either the size of the area or move it somewhere apart from the center, consult your manual) Again, you will have to read up on your particular camera to see how these modes are named for your model, but on Nikons they are called Matrix, Center Weighted, and Spot respectively.

Matrix metering looks at the lighting dispersed evenly throughout the frame. This mode is good for evenly lit scenes, but its' use is fairly limited for our purposes. Center weighted does take the whole scene into account but does just what the name says, it pays a lot more attention to the center portion of your composition and tilts the exposure recommendation to make sure that center area will be properly exposed even at the expense of the periphery. Spot metering takes this one step further. The camera meter will recommend a proper exposure for whatever is at a small, clearly defined center point of the image (unless your camera allows you to designate a spot other than the center) and sacrifice the rest of the frame. Later on you will see examples of each of these modes in action.

Regardless of mode, your meter will only give you a best guess at what it thinks is the proper exposure based on the comparison of what it sees to the internal database. The theater environment is very difficult for your camera meter as it often presents wild extremes of light- like a performer under a brilliant while spotlight surrounded by a completely black stage. I will discuss later how to work around this, but for now there is one more concept we need to talk about - Exposure Compensation

Your camera has a way for you to set an Exposure Compensation factor into its' meter calculations. If shoot at what your meter says is the proper exposure but your images come out consistently too bright, you can dial in a negative exposure compensation as a meter correction. If the "proper" shots come out too dark, you can dial in a positive exposure compensation value. You can generally adjust this in either 1/3, 1/2 or full stop increments and there will be some sort of indicator in your viewfinder to remind you that you are using this setting. Basically you can think of Exposure Compensation as a way to quickly and easily calibrate your camera meter to the given conditions you are experiencing. When shooting with any setting in Automatic, EC is the only method you have of effecting the exposure. We will revisit this concept in the settings chapter.

ISOs and Noise

ISO, which is a measurement of your sensors' sensitivity to light, is an acronym for International Standards Organization. When I first started shooting back in the film days there was another acronym for film sensitivity- ASA, or American Standards Association. There were also different organizations in Europe with their own acronyms; ISO consolidated them all and is now the standard measure for both film and digital sensitivity worldwide. In the film days, a given role of film was set to a specific sensitivity by the chemical makeup of its' sensor sites. To get an accurate exposure, you had to tell your camera (and your external light meter, if you used one) what speed your film was. (Speed is the term photographers use to refer to a film's ISO rating). Faster speed films, that is, those with higher ISOs, are more sensitive to light than slower/lower ISO films. (Although I use the past tense here, film is still used and is a very active medium, but this is a book about Digital Photography. I moved from film to digital, so even though film is still present, it's in the past for me.)

In the digital era, the ISO of your camera sensor is not fixed, you can change it on the fly. You could do this to a certain limited extent with film, but you then had to remember you had done it and take care to properly over or under develop the resultant exposures according to how much you had "pushed" your film speed when you shot. In digital photography you don't have to worry about that, you just change the ISO in your camera and shoot, you can use a different ISO for every shot you take in a series and (assuming you were able to get a good exposure for that ISO) they will all come out just as well in your digital darkroom processing.

Every digital camera will have a range of "native" ISO settings. Native ISO refers to the actual range designed into the sensor. Usually there will be a few settings on the lower and a few on the higher end of your ISO menu that are outside this native range, but these will generally not be as clean and useable as the native ISOs will be. For our purposes, you will need to find out what the highest useable ISO is of your particular camera, which you should be able to do fairly easily with a little time on Google or photography sites like DPreview.com. You won't always have to shoot at the maximum, but unless your theater has a high end lighting setup you will often be pretty close to it, especially if you are shooting an entry level camera and kit lens.

So, higher ISOs mean a more sensitive sensor and a brighter image, but there is always a tradeoff. Higher ISOs mean more noise. Noise is a graininess in your image. In film, this graininess was caused by the sensor sites physically being larger than their lower ISO counterparts so they could absorb more light. In digital sensors, noise is a function of the electronics involved and stray signals. As you increase the sensitivity of your sensor so you can record more light (raise your ISO) you make your sensor more susceptible to these stray signals which contaminate your resultant image. All digital images will have some level of noise, even if it is so low as to be completely unnoticeable. How much noise you are comfortable with in your images depends on your personal taste and how you intend to use the images. As long as you determine and stay under the highest useable ISO for your camera, the resultant noise should be within acceptable levels, and there are ways to reduce noise using image processing software later on your computer. I will discuss these techniques farther on in this book.

If you are wondering what excessive noise looks like, here is an example. This is my son, sleeping, the only light in the room is from the streetlights outside the window filtering in through closed blinds. This image is way to noisy to be useable, but I took it just to test the high ISO performance of a new camera (D4) in a pitch dark bedroom at night. This was taken at ISO 204,500 - the highest native ISO on the D4 is 12,800, so that is what I set as maximum for real world shooting. This is just to let you see that just because your camera can shoot at some really high ISOs if you really need the shot, it isn't a great idea to crank it up all the way if you want good images.

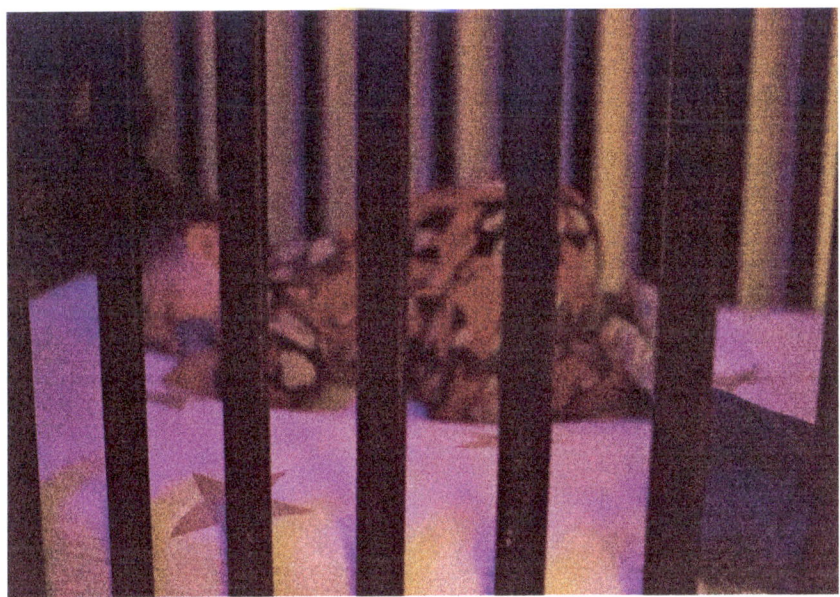

The final note on ISOs and Noise is that not all images shot at the same ISO and settings will have the same apparent level of noise. Noise is most visible in uniform color areas of your image, and the lower the overall exposure the more apparent the noise will appear. Ultimately you will have to experiment with your particular camera at various ISOs in different lighting conditions to get a feel for how noisy your images will be in a particular situation.

Shutter Speed

Finally, an easy one. Shutter speed is a measure of exactly how long your shutter remains open and therefore how long your sensor is exposed to light. Shutter speed is measured in fractions - 1/125 sec, 1/60sec, etc. A larger number on the bottom of the fraction represents a faster shutter speed, 1/125 sec is a faster shutter speed than 1/60 sec, so the shutter is open for less time and therefore less light has time to make it to the sensor. Most DSLRs actually have a two part shutter, each part is called a curtain. The shutter movement occurs in two parts: First the front curtain opens, then the second- or rear- curtain closes. For our purposes you don't need to worry about that, it only becomes important when you are using either a flash or a studio strobe, but you won't be doing that for shooting your child's show (at least I hope you won't after reading this book).

What you need to know for our purposes is that faster shutter speeds let in less light but also take a picture faster. This means that there is less chance of motion blur at faster shutter speeds and you are better able to freeze fast moving subjects. Most DLSRs these days can shoot at up to 1/4000th or 1/8000th of a second if there is enough light. At these speeds blades of a fan would appear to be motionless and no motion blur would happen in any of your shots of your child's performance. Sadly, unless your child is performing outdoors on an open stage in the middle of a bright summer day you won't have enough light to shoot at these speeds. Just like we saw with ISO, there is always a catch and a trade off. For any given set of other settings, a faster shutter speed will better freeze motion but your images will be darker. You will have to determine the slowest shutter speed you need to freeze the motion in your child's show to a level you like. This doesn't mean you have to totally stop the action, a little motion blur is an artistic choice you have to make for yourself. If it's a dance show, for example, and your child is doing a twirl, you could find an appropriate shutter speed that would let you freeze your dancer's face as they spot the turn but would show a slight blur of the arms and legs as they twirl and give a sense of motion. When we see pictures of things that we know are supposed to be moving, it can look strange if there is entirely no motion blur at all. For instance, if you ever see a picture of a helicopter in flight, you will usually find that the photographer left a little bit (or even a lot) of blur in the rotors. Any DSLR out there is capable of shooting fast enough in daylight to completely freeze the motion of the blades, but those images will subconsciously look strange to you because your brain understands that if the rotors ever stopped moving in flight the helicopter would fall out of the air. You also frequently see a type of intentional motion blur used when shooting auto races, or any other sport where speed is a key element. (This typically a type of motion blur effect called panning, and I will explain it in the pro techniques section)

The slower the shutter speed, on the other hand, the more light can get to the sensor and the brighter your shot will be. Most cameras can slow down to about a 30 second exposure. Note that was not 1/30 sec but thirty seconds. There is also a setting called "B" or Bulb. A holdover from a device used in the old film days to trigger extra long exposures, this means that as long as you hold the shutter button down, the shutter will stay open. In the old days you literally hooked a bulb syringe up to the shutter release, and squeezed the bulb to fire the shutter using air pressure, which would stay open until you released the bulb. This gentle use of air to activate the shutter prevented the camera from shaking like it would if you pressed the button by hand. These bulbs were replaced with cable releases, which served the same function. Today's DSLRs use electronic cable releases or remote controls. If you have a smartphone you can probably find an adapter and an app that will let you control your shutter from your phone or tablet. If you have ever seen star trails or night shots that look bright enough to be daytime, you have seen long exposure shots.

Between those two extremes, what sort of shutter speeds will you need to use to capture your child's performance? It depends on the performance in question and your taste for motion blur. If your star is doing Hamlet's monologue, center stage and relatively stationary with only the occasional hand gesture, you should be fine with 1/100th, maybe 1/80th sec. If your performer is doing a lightening fast tap dance routine or really intricate ballet number, you may need to get up to 1/320th sec or faster, although you may find you like a slower speed that gives a nice blur. I find that for the circus shows I shoot I am usually at 1/250th or 1/320th second and that stops all but the fastest drops. For really dynamic performers doing fast routines, I may go up to 1/500th second.

Aperture and Depth of Field

Aperture is not quite as easy as shutter speed, but is just as important. If you remove your lens from your camera and look at the the back of it, you will see an iris made up of somewhere between 5 - 9 separate sections with a small opening in the center. Aperture is a way of describing the size of that opening. Unless you are using a very unique special purpose lens, you will have a range of apertures you can choose from. An aperture is often referred to as an F-Stop - when you see information on a shot the aperture setting used will be listed as F5.6, F2.8, etc. A higher F-number means a smaller opening, which means less light gets through. A smaller F- number means a larger opening, meaning more light gets through.

When you are shopping for lenses and see them described, you will either see a single aperture- i.e. F2.8 or F1.4 or a variable range of apertures like F3.5-5.6 or similar. Prime lenses have a constant aperture, in the F1.8 range for consumer level lenses and F1.4 or F1.2 for most professional primes. Most consumer and a few professional zooms are variable aperture. For example, a common kit lens is the 18-55mm F3.5-5.6. This means at the widest zoom, 18mm, the lens can open to a maximum aperture of F3.5 but as you zoom in to the 55mm maximum focal length your widest aperture also shrinks down to F5.6. Constant aperture zoom lenses, for example the 24-70mm F2.8, are capable of using the same widest aperture across all their zoom ranges.

Like shutter speed, aperture changes effect the amount of light that is able to pass through to your sensor and thus change the brightness level of your image. Also like shutter speed, there is a trade off. The wider the aperture, the more light gets through, and the brighter your image. However, the wider the aperture goes, the shallower Depth Of Field you will have in your image.

Depth of Field refers to how much of your image (from close to far) is in focus. Shallow depth of field means what you focus on and almost nothing else in front of or behind that point will be in focus. Wide depth of field means that there will be a longer range of area in focus both in front of and behind your subject. If you want to understand the physics behind this concept, there are many web sites that can explain it far better than I can, but what you need to understand is that there are three main factors that effect your depth of field: Aperture, distance from your subject and focal length of your lens. Wider apertures and longer focal lengths (greater zoom) means shallower depth of field. Smaller apertures and wider angle lenses mean greater depth of field. For a given lens/aperture combination, the closer you are to your subject the narrower your effective depth of field will be. If you have ever seen a portrait where only a single eye of the model was in sharp focus and everything else in the image was slightly out of focus, it was most likely shot from close up with a wide aperture and a long focal length lens.

Shallow depth of field. This image was taken with on a D4 (full frame) using an 85mm lens at F1.4, about 10 feet from the subject. If you look closely you will see that her left eye is in sharp focus but the hair, the closer eye and hat brim are out of focus as well as everything in the background.

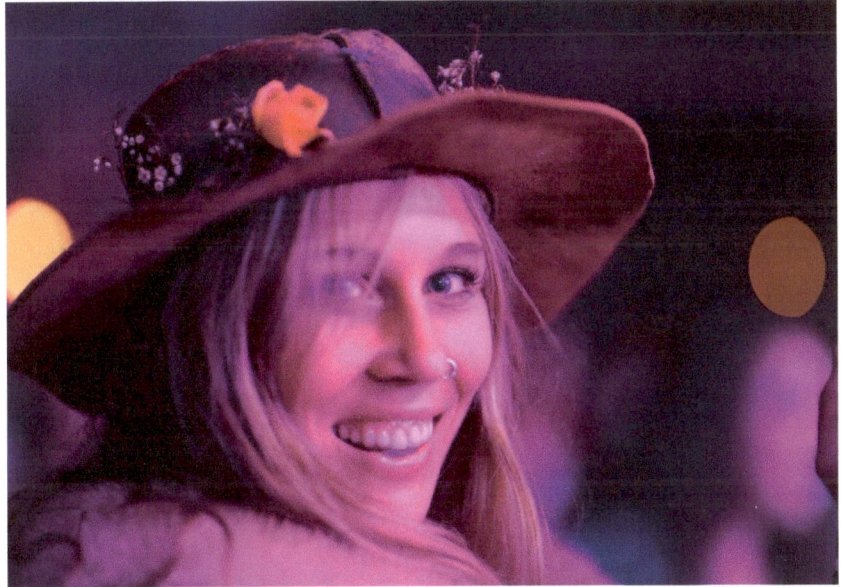

Conversely, if you see a landscape image where everything from the grass in front of the camera to the trees in the distance are in sharp focus, that was most likely captured from a distance with a wide angle lens and a small aperture.

Deep depth of field. This image was shot on a D800 (full frame) using a 14-24mm lens at 24mm, F7.1, and pretty much everything in the image is in focus.

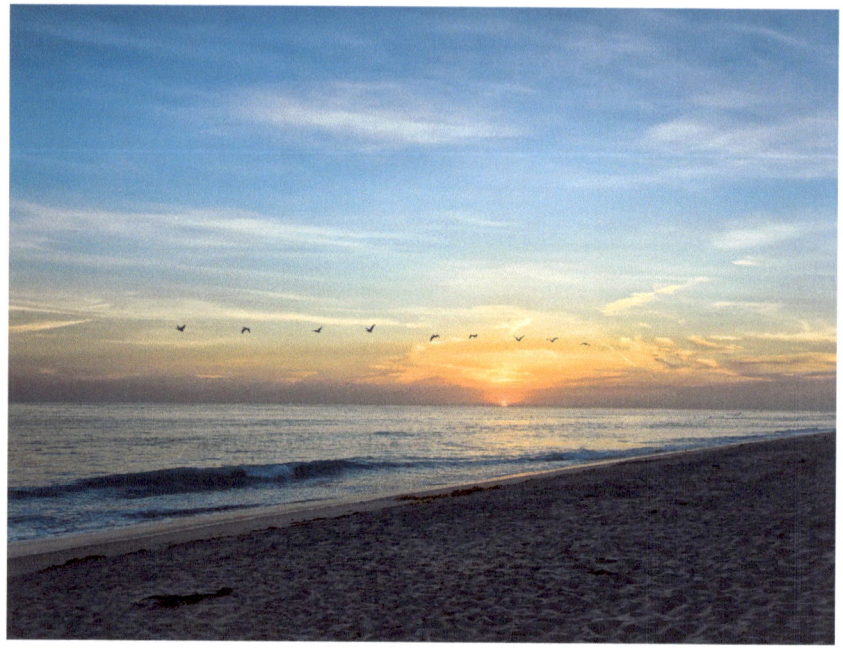

You can find web sites and smart phone applications that will calculate exactly what your depth of field will be for a given camera, lens, aperture and distance from your subject if you really want to geek out. Finally, if all the rest of the factors are the same, the larger your camera sensor, the shallower the depth of field will be. This ability to use really shallow depths of field is another factor that makes larger sensors so important to professional photographers.

If you don't want to geek out, here is how all this effects you: In standard theatrical lighting situations you will most likely be shooting at the widest aperture your lens can support to let in enough light to allow you to use the higher shutter speeds you will need to freeze the action. If you are shooting with a kit lens and can't go wider than F3.5 you will probably have enough depth of field that you won't have to worry about it as long as you only want to focus on your star. If you have multiple children and they are on opposite sides of the stage from you, you may need to use a smaller aperture (larger number) to keep them both in focus. If you are using a fast lens (lenses with wider apertures are referred to as "faster" because you can shoot faster shutter speeds with them) like a pro zoom or an F1.8 prime, you will need to be careful if you shoot wide open. The depth of field with these wide apertures can be inches or less and if you aren't very careful and precise with your focus points you may be disappointed in your results. When I shot the image above at F1.4, I had to pick which eye I wanted in focus and aim my focus point very carefully at that eye.

I find that I get my best results using apertures of F4 - F5.6 when there is enough light to do so. A final note is that each lens will have a certain particular "sweet spot," an aperture usually towards the middle of its' range, at which you will get the sharpest images and the best performance your lens is capable of. A quick internet search will let you find out what that sweet spot is for each of the lenses you carry and use.

Frame Size

The final concept I will discuss for your background knowledge is frame size. You will frequently hear cameras described as "full frame," or "crop sensor." In the Nikon world these are referred to as FX (full) or DX (crop), other manufacturers will have their own particular designations for their camera models. DSLR cameras are based on their film camera ancestors, so a full frame DSLR quite simply has a sensor that is roughly the same dimensions as a single frame of 35mm film. Any DSLR with a sensor smaller than this size is referred to as a "crop" sensor. Nikon DX cameras have a 1.5x crop factor, in other words, the sensor is 3/4 the size of a 35mm film frame or full frame sensor. I think Canon uses a 1.6 crop factor, you can look up the particular number for your camera if you are so inclined. Point and shoot cameras will almost all have a smaller sensor than the crop sensor DSLRs, while medium and large format cameras have substantially larger sensors. (and correspondingly larger price tags- go look at the Hasselblad catalogue if you want to get an example)

As I discussed in the earlier chapter on how your camera sees; for a given resolution, a larger sensor will function better in low light than a smaller one. The trade off is that, for any given feature level, the larger the sensor the more expensive the camera will be. The larger sensor also gives a more shallow depth of field for any given focal length lens and aperture setting.

The other main factor you need to be aware of is lens selection. Traditional lens focal length descriptions are standardized to their field of view on a traditional 35mm film camera. Thus, a 50mm lens on a full frame DSLR will behave like a 50mm lens on a traditional film camera. If you put the same 50mm lens on a crop sensor camera, you will get a tighter field of view. To determine the field of view you will see with your camera/lens combination, you need to multiply the focal length of the lens by the crop factor of your sensor. If you put that 50mm lens on a Nikon DX camera with a 1.5 crop, you would wind up with the same field of view as a 75mm lens on a full frame camera. (50 x 1.5 = 75). NOTE: Lenses that are specifically designed for crop sensor cameras will accurately list their focal length, no multiplication necessary. Each manufacturer will have their own code to designate these lenses. Nikon calls these DX lenses as well. This means a 50mm DX lens on a Nikon DX camera will have the same field of view as a regular 50mm lens on a Nikon FX camera.

You will often hear this mentioned as one advantage of the crop sensor, since it increases the apparent magnification of your lenses. This isn't entirely true, if you took a shot with the 50mm lens on the full frame camera, loaded it into your computer and manually cropped out the edges of the image to a size equal to the crop factor, you would see the same image you would get putting the 50mm lens on the crop sensor camera. Further discussion of this is way beyond the scope of this book; for our purposes if you put a lens designed for a full frame camera onto a crop sensor camera, it will effectively behave like a slightly longer lens.

All pre-DSLR lenses for 35mm cameras are designed for 35mm film, and are thus full frame lenses. All the major camera manufacturers make lenses specifically designed for their crop sensor cameras. If you have a crop sensor lens, it will behave like you would expect from its' marked focal length when you use it on your cropped sensor camera. What happens when you put a crop sensor lens on a full frame camera? This is another time where I cannot give a one size fits all answer. On Nikon FX cameras the camera will recognize the DX lens and, unless you tell it otherwise, will automatically crop your images to match the field of view of the lens. If you choose to override this automatic setting, you will find that you will have vignetting on your images. (Vignetting is the technical term for borders around your image, in this case black areas where your lens didn't allow light to fall on the sensor).

If you are just starting out you probably have an entry level crop frame

DSLR and crop lenses to match up with it. If you decide to expand your photographic horizons, start by investing in high quality, professional caliber full frame lenses. They will give you increased capability on your crop sensor camera, and will be fully compatible if you decide later on to upgrade to a full frame camera. If you plan to stick with crop sensor cameras, there are a few incredible, professional lenses designed for crop sensor cameras on the market as well.

Image Format

DSLRs have multiple choices when it comes to how you would like your images saved. The two you are most likely to see are raw and JPEG. Some cameras may also offer TIFF, but that is rare (for in camera capture at least) and I won't talk about it here. Just know it exists and you may see that option again when we talk about post processing. If you have a point and shoot camera, unless it is a higher end one, you will only have the option of JPEG. (If you see JPG that is the same as JPEG for out purposes). Within each main type you will have some level of quality or size settings.

Raw is not a specific image format in and of itself. Shooting in raw means the camera is going to record everything it sees when the image is taken and save it all as a file to pull off your camera later with no processing done to the data in camera. Each manufacturer and often each specific camera model will have its' own specific raw file output with its' own suffix. Nikon raw files, for example, will be somename.NEF files. However, the .NEF file from a D4 will be different from the .NEF file from a D3300 and so on. If you think of your final picture as a pizza, the raw image format is like a grocery cart containing all the ingredients. When you choose to record images in your camera's raw file format, what you download onto your computer afterwards is like the dough, pepperoni, cheese, and various toppings all in a bag that you would bring home from the store. Once you get home, you can take all those ingredients and combine them in almost any way you like and bake them up however you would like to make various styles of pizza. If you don't use all the ingredients the first time, you can come back and make a new pizza from them later using a different recipe that you may like better. If you shoot in your camera's raw format you may have a choice of different bit levels. You don't really need to understand what that means, just know that the higher the bit level the more data is recorded and the more options you will have later.

JPEG on the other hand, is a specific image format, and can be thought of as a finished pizza. In this analogy, your camera is like your local pizza shop. The settings you have dialed into the camera are the toppings you are going to get on your pizza, and clicking the shutter is like calling in your order. Downloading your images off the camera is like getting your pizza delivered, if you don't like what you got, too bad, it's what you ordered and it's too late to change it. You can season it a little and add garnish with parmesan or peppers, but if you want something completely different you have to go back and start over by ordering something new from the pizza store. What this means is that if you save in JPEG format, your camera will process the image itself, using whatever settings you have chosen, save the result and discard the rest of the image data. This will limit your post processing options later on. If you choose to shoot JPEG you will have options for quality and size to choose from. The larger and higher quality options record more information than the smaller and lower quality choices.

The raw vs JPEG debate has been going on for a while and shows no sign of slowing down, a quick trip to Google will get you more than you ever want to read on the topic. Reading my description above, you may think that obviously, since shooting in raw gives you more options, it's always better. This is true in theory, but like everything else we have discussed, in reality there are trade offs. Since raw is not actually an image format, before you can use any images you shot in raw you need to convert them. This means you cannot take them straight out of the camera and post them onto a web site, email them to friends and family, or send them to the print shop. You have to open them in some form of image converter, decide which settings you like, and convert them. Keeping with the pizza analogy, you can't just come home from the supermarket and eat, you have to get home, mix the ingredients and bake the pizza first. Also, just like that bag of groceries takes up more space than the finished pizza, raw files are generally much larger than their JPEG counterparts, so you need larger memory cards in your camera and more space on your computer to process them later on. JPEG files, on the other hand, are smaller and more convenient. They don't take up as much space, and just like that delivery pizza, they are ready to go as soon as you get them. You can take them straight out of the camera and use them however you want to immediately since they are finished image files. As long as you got your order pretty close to how you like, you can add a little bit of seasoning if you need it (ie- you can still edit JPEG images after they are shot, just nowhere near the level you can with a raw file) and as long as it tastes good you are all set.

That's all you need to know for now, I will cover my personal recommendations in the camera settings chapter coming up in the next section.

Camera Settings

Now that you have a basic understanding of the terminology I will be using for the rest of the book, we're ready to discuss how to set up your camera to actually shoot your child's performance.

Flash

I will get this out of the way first since it is the easiest. TURN YOUR FLASH OFF! It's that simple. There are really only two situations I will recommend you use a flash, and I will mention those later, but in general it is a bad idea for theater photography. First and foremost, if your child is doing a dance number or something similarly complex and possibly dangerous like the circus performers I shoot, flash can be a potentially deadly distraction. You would feel pretty bad if you blinded your kid at a critical moment as they were spotting a turn and were the cause of a sprained ankle and an embarrassing fall on stage right? It's just not worth it. Second, unless you are really proficient at using your flash to augment the scene, your images will not look as good as they would if you just shot in the light that's already there. Third, speaking of the light that is already there, someone most likely spent a lot of time and energy to design the lighting for the performance in such a way that it would enhance the mood of the scene and be a large part of the performance. Blasting away with your flash and hiding their work not only makes your images look flat and washed out but is also highly disrespectful to these artists. Finally, it is also disrespectful to everyone else who is trying to take pictures of their children. You will understand this the first time you look at what otherwise would have been a perfectly timed and exposed image of your child that has been ruined by someone else's flash going off at precisely the wrong time and destroying your shot.

This is what happens when someone else's flash goes off during your shot.

Same subject and settings as the blowout shot above, this is what is was supposed to look like (even though this wasn't a keeper shot by a long shot, just here so you can see the contrast with the blowout one)

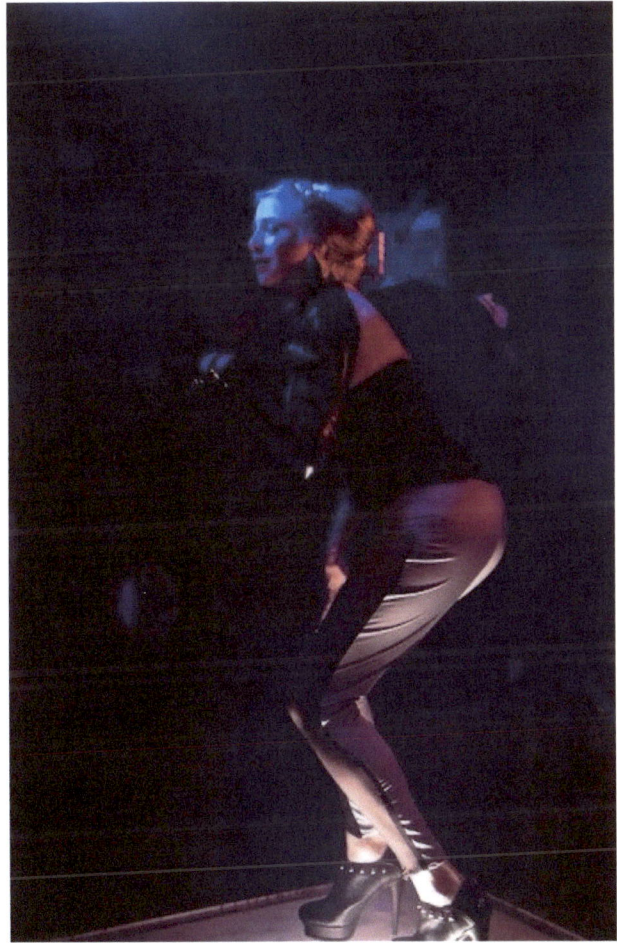

Ok- so I said there are only two situations where you would want to use flash. The first situation is for an outdoor, open air performance in the middle of a sunny day when there is no additional stage lighting being used. This seems counter intuitive at first, because to your eye it looks like there is plenty of light and everything is fine. When you look at your images; however, since your camera cannot automatically adjust for the range between light and dark as well as your eyes can, you will probably notice that your images are full of areas that are too bright mixed with deep dark shadows that hide eyes (especially if your star's costume includes a hat with any sort of brim). In this case, the only thing you can do is add a little fill flash to brighten (fill) in those shadows.

In this situation, unless you are sitting in the front row, the built in popup flash on your DSLR won't have the power or range to help out very much, although it's better than nothing if it's all you have. An external hot shoe flash is a lot better, the best case is if you can put it somewhere off your camera and remote trigger it, but that is a more advanced technique. For our purposes, I will assume you are using either your pop-up or an external hot shoe flash attached to your camera. In either case, I recommend that you use the lowest power setting possible that will give enough light to eliminate shadows. To get the most control over this you would need to put your flash in manual, take test shots and manually reduce the power as low as you can while still getting the results you want. Once you are set you don't need to change anything unless you or your move closer or farther apart. The simplest way; however, is to leave your flash in automatic and use something called Flash Exposure Compensation to increase or reduce flash output. I will talk about camera exposure compensation later, but when it comes to Flash EC, just understand that it is separate from Camera EC, and only effects the level of the flash contribution to the overall exposure. Every positive full stop of Flash EC doubles the amount of flash power, every negative full stop halves it. Flash exposure controls, modes and labels vary widely between manufacturers, so you will have to consult both your camera manual and your flash manual to learn how yours works. Different camera and flash systems have different types of automatic modes (by the way, if you buy a less expensive external flash from a third party manufacturer, you may be limited to manual mode only) but for the most part these will be labeled as some variation of TTL (through the lens) meaning they use a system of pre-flashes to set flash exposure based on your camera's meter readings. A full explanation of how TTL works is far beyond our purposes, but most TTL systems will generally work pretty well as long as you remember to set your meter up properly, which will be discussed later.

Here is an example of a shot using fill flash. This was an outdoor performance in the early afternoon. The stage lights were focused for the band and did not light the aerial performance area. If I had not used the fill flash here, I would have had to choose between exposing for the face and blowing out everything else, or exposing for the sunlit areas and her face would have been lost in shadow. In these conditions since the eyes are already adapted, flash isn't as potentially dangerous to use.

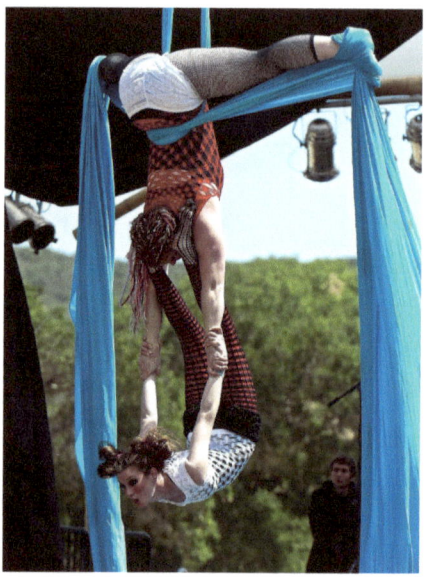

The second situation where you may have no choice but to use flash is when you are in a very dark space and the lighting guy simply gave up, or there was no budget or thought to lighting. For most school and dance studio shows, you will be fine with the light that is available. On the other hand, if your child is older and happens to be doing stand up at the local open mic night at your neighborhood tavern, it may just be too dark to get good shots no matter how good your gear is. When you have to get the shot and there is no other choice, make sure your performer and anyone else they are sharing the stage with won't mind, and use your flash. Again, you want to use it at the lowest power level you can use that will allow you to get your shot. If you think you will be in this situation, take some time to learn about off camera flash, or at least diffusers and bounce flash options, but those options won't be needed by most of you.

Here is an example of this situation. It was at an outdoor performance at night, the lighting system that was supposed to light the aerial rig never arrived, so there was no light at all on the performers. I talked to them and told them if they wanted any images I would have to use flash, and they were ok with it, so I did.

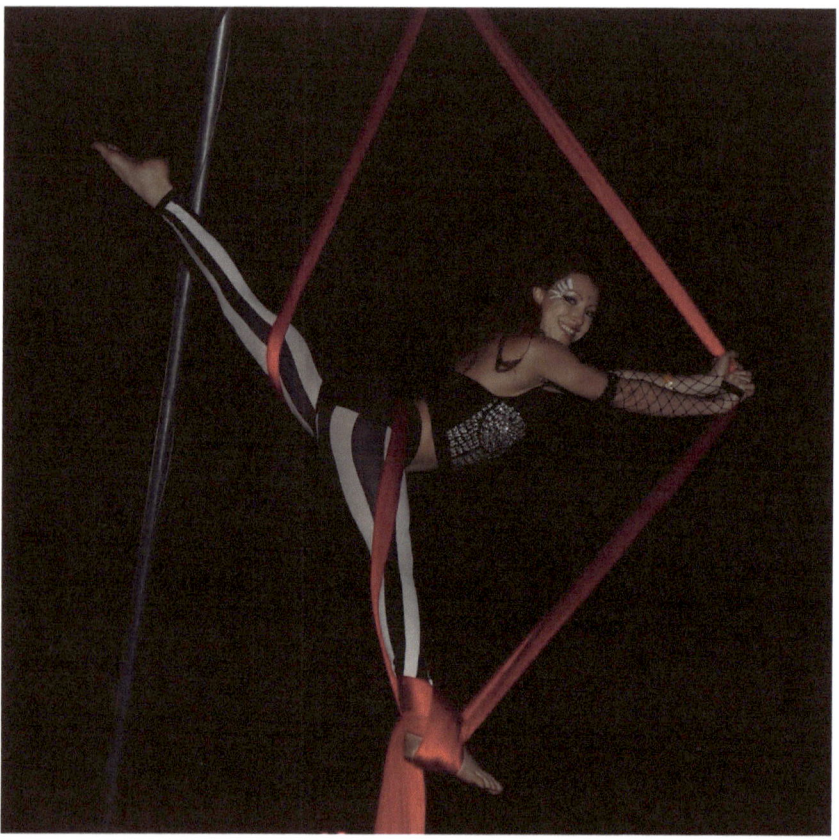

There are a few other techniques where flash can be useful, but unless your child is a polynesian fire twirler those situations are also beyond the scope of this book. (If you do have a need to shoot fire spinners, drop me an email and I'll talk your ear off about it) I do need to leave you with one other warning about flash-unless your camera and flash combination offer some form of High Speed synchronization option (Nikon calls this Auto FP High Speed Sync) then as soon as you turn on a flash your shutter speed will be limited to a maximum. Most entry level DSLRs do not offer the high speed sync option and have a maximum flash synchronization speed of around 1/200 Sec. Discussing what this means and how it works is beyond the scope of this book, if you are using the flash in a dark room it probably won't matter because the quick light from the flash (which becomes the only light source in the shot effectively) will serve to freeze motion for you, but if you are using the flash as a daytime fill light this limit may keep you from shooting fast enough to eliminate motion blur while you use your flash. If you shoot your flash in manual and notice a black bar across one side of your image, you are trying to shoot faster than your camera's highest flash synchronization speed. Again, it's too much for this book to get into, but if it happens to you I just want you to know what to search for online to see what is happening and why.

LCD Preview Screen

OFF. This one is simple. You want that bright screen on the back of your camera to be off by default and to only turn on when you have a real need to use it. Otherwise the light from it will distract others around you from enjoying their kids' performances. Looking at the preview images on the back of the camera after every shot will also distract you, mark you as a amateur, and cause you to miss not only future shots but also your child's show.

Find the settings on your camera that control the LCD screen. First you want to set the brightness level to the dimmest level that will let you see it in the theater. To get an idea of what this level is, turn off the lights in a room with no windows and adjust it there, that should be about right. Next, find a setting called "auto preview" or something similar, and turn it off. This setting controls whether each shot will appear on the screen immediately after you shoot it.

Again, individual options and labels for these menu items will vary between cameras, but the idea is you want to control when that screen is on. When set properly, it will not activate unless you tell it to, whether that is to access the information screen or menus, or you want to look at a specific shot you have taken. I will discuss when to do this when we get to the shooting techniques section.

One final note- if your preview screen offers you the option of turning on "blinkies" you should do so. "Blinky" is the not so technical term for a feature that allows your camera to show you areas of either highlights or shadows that are outside the dynamic range of your camera in your exposure- in other words, blown out. When an area of highlight is blown out, no amount of post production work will be able to recover detail in that area. Small blown out areas are acceptable, but if anything you really want to see is blown out you will have to adjust your exposure and reshoot.

Choosing an ISO

The first step in choosing an ISO is to figure out your camera's highest useable ISO if you have not already done so. The easiest way to do this is by doing a search online and finding research someone else has already done with your make and model of camera. If you want to be more exact or don't want to trust internet information, set yourself up with an experimental staged image and test for yourself.

To test for yourself, find a spot in your home that has even lighting that will not change (ie- a lightbulb, not a window) an ideal place for this will be a bathroom with a towel rack that leaves you room to shoot. You will need a light colored (white or beige) piece of fabric (or a light colored wall will also work) and a dark (blue/brown/black) piece of fabric. Towels will work in a pinch, but a tablecloth or sheet works better because the smoother the texture of your target objects, the easier it will be to see the noise in the resultant image. Maybe all you have isa black plastic waste bin that you can put in front of a white wall, that is fine. What you are looking for is two evenly lit, smooth surfaces, one light and one dark. If you want to add a few other solid colors in addition that is fine as well.

Once you are set up, switch your camera to aperture priority and choose a mid range setting, if there is enough light F5.6 would be perfect but if you have to shoot your lens wide open that's fine. If you have a tripod, break it out and use it. Set your camera to around ISO 400, focus on your target and take a shot. Up your ISO to 800, take a shot, repeat for 1600, 3200, and higher if you have them. You can shoot in either raw or JPEG, whichever you plan to use for your actual shooting later on. If you shoot JPEG be sure to turn off any in camera noise reduction for the first series of shots. If you are going to shoot JPEG or raw + JPEG, repeat the series of shots with the in camera noise reduction turned on and again for each level, so you will also know how effective this function is at various levels and ISOs for your camera. Make sure you write down which set used which settings so you can remember when you go back to examine them.

Move your images onto the computer and open them in your photo viewer/ editor. Zoom in to 100% and look at your images, both the dark areas and the light areas. As the ISOs increase, you will see increased noise, usually it will increase faster on the dark areas than the light, and you will be able to see the level at which you find the noise is too much for your tastes. I will talk later on about post production noise reduction, but if you already know what it is, you can go ahead and use your software to see how capable it is with your images; which may allow you to use higher ISOs comfortably on your camera knowing you can reduce the noise to an acceptable level later on. There is no right answer on how much noise is too much, it's a judgement call on your part, but take a note of which ISO you think is the fastest your camera is capable of, both with and without reduction. (Either in camera or post) Most entry level cameras should be fine up to 1600, or 3200 with noise reduction, but if you have the time to check for yourself it's worth it. You may get better results at higher ISOs than you think.

When it comes time to actually set your ISO for the performance, I will offer you two options, depending on your camera capabilities. All of my cameras have an Auto-ISO setting which lets me specify the maximum setting the camera is allowed to use. My preferred method of shooting shows is to activate the Auto-ISO function and set the cap at that camera's highest useable ISO (this is different on each of my cameras). If this setting is available to you, I recommend you use it. What this allows you to do is set the camera to the shutter speed / aperture combination you want and then the camera will adjust ISO as necessary for a proper exposure (according to its' meter) up to your limit in dark scenes, but if there is more light in a given scene, it will automatically reduce the

ISO and give you less noisy images. The drawback to this method is that if you want to manually adjust exposure, you cannot do it via shutter or aperture settings as the camera will automatically adjust ISO to return to what it thinks is correct, you will only be able to adjust exposures via Exposure Compensation or taking ISO into manual. The advantage is that if you want to change either shutter speed or aperture, you don't have to worry about making corresponding changes to the other settings as long as you remain below the ISO cap.

If you do not have the Auto ISO function or the ability to limit the camera's automatic choices to the highest useable ISO or below, I suggest using manual ISO mode and starting with one setting below your camera's highest useable ISO. When you start taking your first test images (which I will talk about later) during the show, you can adjust up or down as necessary. Once you get your exposures in the ballpark with the right ISO you can then fine tune with shutter speed or aperture as the light changes.

White Balance

The most important thing with this setting is to pick one and stick with it throughout the show. Do not use auto white balance. In a perfect world you would be able to find out what type of lights the theater you will be shooting in uses and set accordingly, but it doesn't make that much difference. If I know that all the lights will be traditional stage lights and there will be no halogen follow spots, I use the tungsten setting. If the lights are mostly LED or the performers I am most interested in capturing will be lit with powerful spotlights, I use the flash setting. (By this I mean the flash white balance setting, I still leave my actual flash off, like we talked about before)

Why not use Auto? If you use auto, the different colors the lighting designer has set on all the lights and scenes throughout the show will make your camera set the white balance to a slightly (or sometimes vastly) different setting from frame to frame. The nice thing about white balance and shooting raw is that if you picked the wrong one, it's pretty easy to change it afterwards in an image editing program. If you used auto white balance, you would have to go through and manually adjust each shot to correct it, but if you shot them all on a single setting and picked wrong, you can edit them all in a batch and change them all to the correct setting in just a few clicks of your editing software.

So, if you know it's primarily Tungsten, pick that and stick with it. LED or follow spot, use Flash WB. For an outdoor show pick either Sun or Cloudy depending on the weather. Whichever you pick, stick with it unless the lighting situation changes, then stick with the new setting as long as your can, that way you can edit in groups if necessary. If you don't know what sort of lighting you will be facing, I suggest using Flash WB.

File Type

This one is easy. If you have a large enough memory card in your camera and enough space on your computer to deal with the images later on, shoot RAW + JPEG Fine (or whatever your camera calls its' highest quality jpeg setting) unless you have a specific reason not to. This combination will give you the most flexibility after the show when it is time to use your images. You will have the JPEG images so that you will be able to email them, post to social media sites, and do anything you need to with them immediately, but if one of your settings didn't work, or you want to go in and do a lot of editing on some particular images later on and make them better, you will have the RAW files to work with, which will give you a lot more flexibility and options when it comes to post production work.

If you are somewhat memory limited (your computer, not trying to insult you here) and don't need the images immediately after the show, shoot RAW. If you are very memory limited, or know you absolutely have no intention of ever opening an image editing program to see what you can do, then shoot JPEG at the highest quality you can that will still give you enough memory space, but I strongly recommend adding RAW to your shooting and at least playing with it later on to see what you can do.

One warning- we'll talk about it later- but I have to mention it now- the preview you see on your camera LCD is always a JPEG using the camera's interpretation. If you shoot raw images and look at them later on the computer, they will look different than you remembered the LCD looking, most likely worse. That is because, unless you have a preset recipe built into your editing software, you aren't seeing the finished image, you are seeing the raw ingredients waiting for you to cook them into something delicious. Again, we'll talk about this later on, I just don't want you to be surprised. This is another reason I recommend shooting RAW + JPEG if you have the memory; that way if you like the way the camera made the pizza you can eat it as it is, if you don't you still have the ingredients to remake it any way you like.

Shooting Mode

Again, you have several options. If you have the Auto-ISO capability I mentioned in the preceding section and have decided to use it, then I suggest setting your camera to Manual mode and selecting your own shutter speed and aperture combination as I will describe later on in sections devoted to those two settings.

If you are using a fixed ISO, you have two options, either shutter priority or aperture priority. You could also still go with full manual and take control of all three variables yourself, but it is easier, especially when starting out, to work with two of the three major settings fixed and having only one variable to deal with. In what I am going to recommend here, I have to tell you that I appear to be in the minority opinion from a quick search online. I recommend that you set your camera to shutter priority mode. Here's why.

Pros that shoot shows in aperture priority are generally shooting fast glass with the ability to go wide open on their lenses and get a resulting very shallow depth of field. They are also mostly shooting from the camera pit right in front of the stage. So, with wide open fast lenses from close up, these pros will have razor thin depths of field at max aperture. If these pros set their camera to shutter priority they would have no control over aperture and the resultant depth of field and thus would not be able to predict in advance how much of a shot would be in focus. They prefer control over depth of field. Also, most pro level cameras let them to specify a lowest allowable shutter speed setting. If this option is available to you on your camera then Aperture priority is definitely a viable option and will give you more control over depth of field and could be a better choice, especially if you have a lens capable of shooting at F1.2, F1.4 or F2.8 and you are shooting from close up.

However, chances are you are that readers of this book will be shooting on a crop sensor camera with a kit lens and from the middle or back of the audience. If the widest your aperture can open up is F3.5 and you are sitting 20 feet from the stage, you will have plenty of depth of field to work with unless you are trying to get the whole stage in focus at once. Your main concern will be to make sure you are using a fast enough shutter speed to freeze motion. If you are in shutter priority with a fixed ISO set, as it gets darker your aperture will open up, and you will have less depth of field, but in most circumstances this will not be an issue for you. For example, let's say you are shooting with the low end Nikon D3300 and its' kit 18-55mm F3.5-F5.6mm lens. You are roughly 20ft from your superstar, so you will probably be using the 55mm end of your zoom range, which means the widest your lens can open is F5.6. With these variables, you have a depth of field of 9 ft, 6.3 in. This is plenty to capture your superstar. Let's say you wanted to zoom out and get the whole cast, so you took your lens to the 18mm setting and it opened up to its' widest aperture of F3.5. With these settings, everything from 8 feet away from you out to the back wall of the theater (or the horizon if you were outdoors) would be in focus, so I think you would be ok. If you stay in shutter priority and the lights on the stage get brighter, your camera will automatically choose a smaller aperture (larger number, remember) and you will get even better depth of field and you will also have the option of lowering your shutter speed to brighten your shots. (If you want to know, I got these numbers using the "Simple DoF" iPad application)

If you used aperture priority without the ability to set a low shutter speed limit for your camera, as it got darker your camera would select slower and slower shutter speeds and you would most likely wind up with too much motion blur and useless images. So, if you are a pro or advanced amateur who knows what you are doing and why (you wouldn't be reading this book anyway) then use aperture priority if it is appropriate for you, but for those of you just starting out, I recommend you stick with shutter speed priority.

To sum if up- if you are shooting Auto ISO, I recommend Manual mode, if you are using a fixed ISO I recommend shutter priority. Whichever way you go, I will discuss how to pick your shutter speed for either mode in a later section. Just remember that if you shoot in a priority mode you will probably not see your exposure meter bars unless you dial in exposure compensation.

Metering Modes

We touched on the concept of metering modes earlier, but here is where we will get into detail so you will know which to pick and why. But first I want you to set up another test. (If you don't feel like being scientific yourself, I will put some results in for you in a bit) The easiest way to set this test up is to find a dark background, preferably a black wall. If you don't have a black wall, use a black sheet and hang it up somewhere. The important thing is that you have a black or very dark background that will completely fill your frame to simulate a dark theater. A small black backdrop won't work, you need the subject to be relatively small in comparison, like they would be if they were standing alone on a stage. For a subject, get your significant other or your kid (if they can stand still for a bit) and put them in an outfit which is a starkly different color tone from their skin and have them stand in front of your black backdrop. Set your camera to its' program mode or either aperture or shutter priority. First, set your camera to matrix metering, focus on your subjects face and take a shot. Without changing anything else, put your camera on center weighted mode. First, focus on your subjects face and take a shot, then focus on the subjects shirt and take another. Switch your metering mode to spot and take another shot focused on the face and another on the shirt. Move these shots into your computer and take a look at the results.

Chances are that on the matrix metered shot your camera adjusted and overexposed your subject's face due to the predominance of darkness in the frame. (If it didn't, please email me and tell me what camera you have, because I want one) The rest of the shots should be pretty close to each other and better exposed for your subject, but depending on how different the color of your subjects shirt is from their skin tone, the center weighted shot focused on the shirt will probably be a better exposure for the face than the spot metered shot focused on the shirt. On the other hand, the spot meter shot focused on the face might be a better exposure for the face but the shirt is either over or under exposed.

There are a lot of variables in this experiment, so just in case your results don't quite line up with what I am trying to demonstrate, here are a series of images that show what I am talking about. I didn't have a model handy, so I just put a dark shirt up against a light background. Most theater scenarios are the opposite; you are focusing on a light performer against a background of darkness, but the effect is easier to see in the reverse.

First we see the Matrix Mode. Exposure is balanced between the light background and the dark shirt, though neither is perfect.

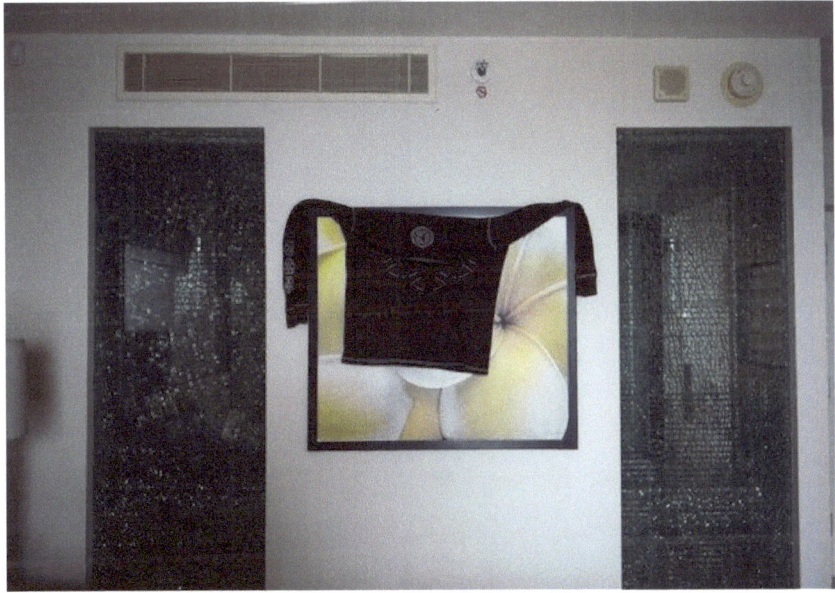

Next I switched to Center Weighted. If you look closely, everything is slightly darker because while the camera was trying to keep everything balanced it was weighted towards the darker shirt in the center.

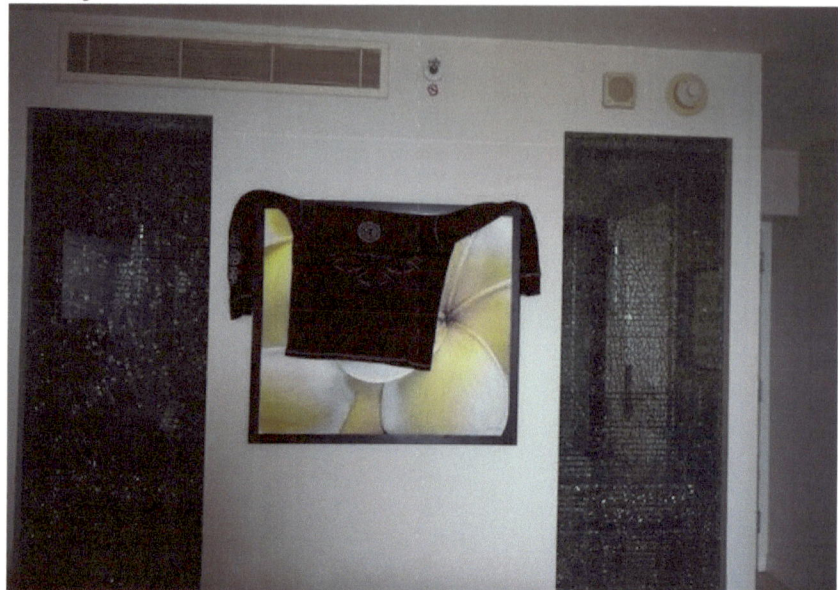

Finally, spot metered on the shirt. Notice how everything is brighter and how blown out the wall is, because the camera got the shirt right at the expense of the rest of the images. This will generally be fine in reverse because it will only make the black background darker.

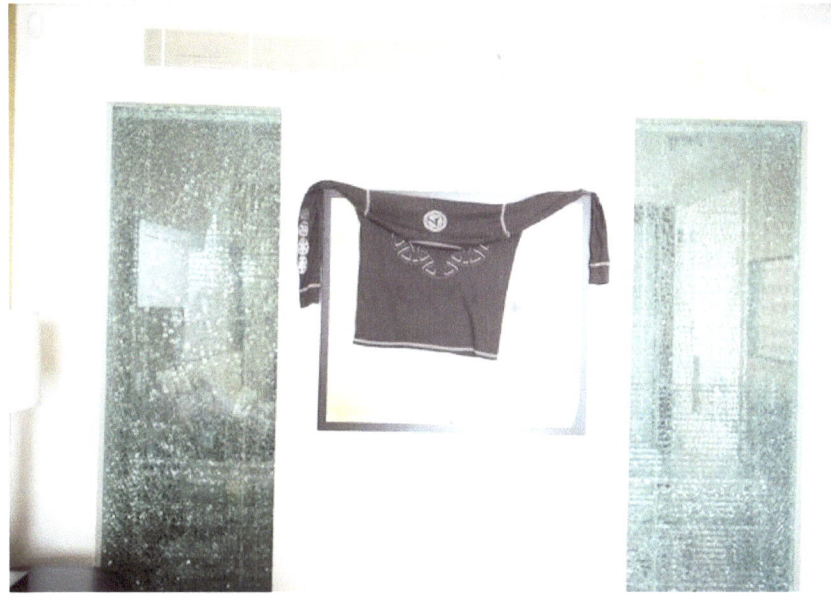

So, now you have seen at least one demonstration, hopefully two, of how the different metering modes can effect your shooting. For most theater scenarios that you will be facing I recommend using spot metering, as this will give the most consistent good results. As always, there are exceptions to every rule- but unless you find yourself in one of these situations, spot is the way to go. If you don't see the results you want, try center weighted, but in general spot metering will be your best bet, as long as you remember to put the meter on the brightest spot, (usually your star's face) or the most important to have properly exposed if this isn't the brightest spot. (You might face that scenario if your performer is wearing all white, or even worse, a metallic gold or silver costume- in this case you may need to meter off the costume)

The special circumstance I'll talk about is if you are shooting that outdoor, brightly lit show on sunny day and using fill flash. In this case the matrix mode will probably be your best bet, especially if you use your flash in the automatic mode. Actually, if you are trying use a TTL flash as a fill, you will probably get strange results unless you are in matrix mode. If you use a TTL flash system in center or spot mode, the flash will give a great output and properly expose for your star's face (or whatever else you are focused on) but the rest of your frame will probably be horribly underexposed.

Again, this is important enough that I will repeat it, whether you are using center weighted or spot metering, it is very important that you focus on the area of the image that is most important to have properly exposed, which will generally be your superstar's face. If you put the meter point somewhere else it can throw off your exposure, especially if you happen to meter on that black background. You might want to deviate from this every one in a while for a little creative expression. If there is a bright background (or a light behind your superstar, you can try a shot with the meter aimed at that bright spot, which should result in you getting a fun silhouette of your superstar.

In this image I metered for the white wall in the background knowing the performer close to me would become a silhouette.

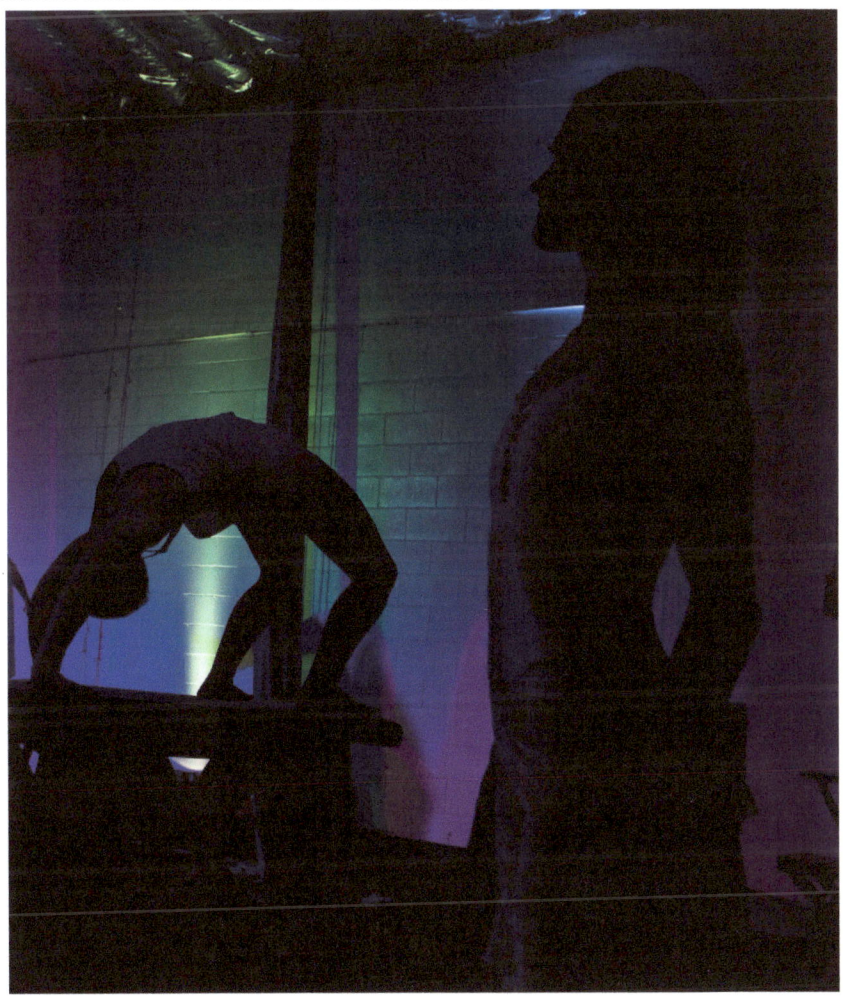

Drive Mode

Most cameras will offer you either two or three options. The first will be single shot, where you get one shot for each press of the shutter button. The other modes will be continuous- you hold down the shutter button and the camera will shoot multiple frames at whatever its' set rate is until either you release the button or the memory buffer fills up. Depending on your camera you may have one continuous mode or more than one choice with varying frame rate options. You may even be able to vary these frame rates further using your menus.

I recommend single shot. While the machine gun approach seems easier, unless you have properly timed the shot (as we will discuss in the techniques section) shooting in continuous will probably only result in you winding up with an image right before and right after the moment you wanted to capture. A misconception is that shooting with the continuous shutter option will work like a movie and you won't miss anything. This is not the case. Movies are shot anywhere from 24-60 frames per second, or even faster for some special effects stuff. The fastest continuous modes out there for DSLRs only get up to 11 or 12 frames per second, not even half the slowest movie speed. And those are the real high end DSLRs, most entry level cameras will cap out at around 4 - 6 frames per second. I learned this when I tried to shoot archery the first time with the D4. I set it to max continuous frame rate and started each burst right before the archer released, but even then would only capture the arrow in flight once in a while. After I got over my annoyance with this and stopped to think about it, it made sense. The arrows were leaving the bow at a speed of approximately 200 feet per second. Even though I was shooting at a shutter speed of 1/8000sec, the frame rate was still 10 frames per second, so one frame every 1/10 second, which meant that the arrows were traveling 20 feet between each shutter snap, even at the fastest speed the best DSLR out there at the time could muster. Maybe your performer isn't moving quite that fast, but you would be surprised how quickly dancers are moving, so if you are only getting 6 frames per second from your camera, therefore a shot every 1/6 of a second, there will be significant motion between your frames and you will only catch the moment you want by luck.

Machine gun mode also fills up your memory card faster and leaves you with a much longer job of going through your images later and picking out the good one from the set of however many you shot in that burst. It also increases the noise your camera makes and thus increases the chance you will annoy those sitting around you.

Finally, no matter how big your memory card is, your camera will only be able to save images to it at a set rate, and this rate will always be slower than the rate you can take images in continuous mode. Your camera gets around this by storing images in a memory buffer until it can write them to your card. If you are familiar with computers, this is analogous to using faster RAM to work on files, then storing them to the comparatively slower hard drive when you are done. The size of your buffer (how many images it can hold) will vary greatly depending on your camera and the file type you are shooting. To give you an example, with my D3200, shooting raw I could only shoot 7 frames before the buffer was full. On my D4, it takes 70 raw images to fill the buffer. Regardless of how many shots it takes to fill your buffer, once you fill it you cannot take another shot until the images in the buffer finish writing to your card. Since most of you will be shooting, at least initially, with entry level cameras, you will probably have smaller buffers. This means that if you shoot machine gun style, you may fill your buffer on one sequence only to spend the next beautiful moment pushing the shutter button and cursing when nothing happens because your camera needs to clear buffer space before it can shoot again.

So, unless you are looking to capture a specific sequence, like a series of turns across the floor by a ballerina, I recommend single shot mode. Actually, I would still recommend it for those floor turns since you would be able to time your shutter firing as your dancer spotted each turn, but until you practice and get your timing down, you might want to go machine gun for this sort of scenario, otherwise single frame remains the best option.

Focus Mode

Sticking with the common theme of this book, I have to warn you that for each different brand of camera, there will be a slightly different set of names used for the various focus options your camera has. Once again, I will discuss these features using the Nikon terminology but there should be similar options on your camera and a quick trip into your manual or a web search should clarify any confusion about what is what. There are three basic focus mode options that your camera should have. The first is Manual Focus, which is exactly what it sounds like. Sometimes this mode is selected on the camera, sometimes on the lens, sometimes on both/either. A manual focus setting on your lens (or using a lens that does not offer auto focus as an option) will always override an autofocus setting on your camera. The other two options are different modes of auto focus. One option will be single, or one time, autofocus. Nikon refers to this as AF-S. Basically this mode means that the instant you push your shutter button halfway, the camera will focus on your designated focus point and after that initial focus will not shift or change focus as long as you keep the shutter button halfway pressed, or until you activate the shutter. This mode is useful if you need to focus and recompose (this means you focus on something in the center of your frame but then move your frame so that the subject is off center, but still in focus). The other main mode is continuous autofocus. Nikon refers to this mode as AF-C. In this mode, the camera will still focus immediately on whatever it is aimed at when you half press the shutter, but in this mode as you move your focus point around while keeping the shutter button depressed, your focus will shift as your aim shifts.

Within the continuous autofocus settings there will be a range of options, again what is available to you will depend on your camera. Generally the options will be single point continuous focus, multi point continuous focus, or all focus point continuous focus. In single point continuous mode the autofocus system will keep whatever is under your chosen focus point in focus as you move the focus point around. In either multi-point or all point continuous mode, the camera's AF system will attempt to figure out what you are actually trying to focus on when you initially focus, then attempt to track that subject as it moves through the range of your chosen focal points. There are more names and varieties of these various sub modes than I could describe here, you will have to consult your camera manual to find out what your options are.

For theatrical photography I definitely recommend using the continuous auto focus mode. Within that main mode, my recommendation is to use either single point or the setting (however your camera labels it) that allows you to use continuous AF with a small cluster of points centered around your chosen focus point. For my Nikon cameras, my preferred mode is AF-C with the D9 (nine point) option. You probably have a method (knob, dial or buttons) with which to move your focus point from the center to one of the other points on your view screen. How many placement choices you have depends on your camera. In general for the beginning shooter I recommend leaving your focus point set to the center. Usually this will be the most accurate focus point, and it is where you will naturally aim the camera at your target. If you forget you have moved your focus point off center and instinctively aim your center point at your child when you see a big moment, you will wind up with an out of focus image. (Technically the image will be in focus, just on the point actually designated, not the one you intended). Keeping your focus point centered just makes things easier and less confusing. As you get more fluid and confident in your camera skills, by all means feel free to experiment and see how changing focus points works for you.

One other setting that Nikons (and I assume other cameras) provide for continuous AF tracking is a delay setting. This delay can be set to various ranges from short to long. This controls how reactive your AF tracking is- how long it waits when either your focus point or your subject moves before it refocuses. If you know your superstar will be the only one on stage when you are shooting, as in a dance solo, set this delay to its' shortest setting so your AF will instantly track as they move. If there will be more people on stage with your child, I recommend setting this to normal or even slightly delayed. This minimizes the chance that your camera will try to instantly refocus on a new subject each time someone else dances or moves in front of your child.

Exposure Compensation

We covered how to read your camera's meter and exposure values already. Basically, the easiest way to understand exposure compensation is that it changes the zero point on your camera's exposure meter up or down by your chosen amount of compensation. In other words, if you set the EC to +1, the your meter will give you a zero reading at one stop brighter than it would otherwise give you the zero, or opposite for negative EC.

This setting is the only way to change exposure if you are using any mode other than full manual. If the camera is allowed to automatically choose ISO, Shutter speed or Aperture, as you change one value it will change another to return to what it thinks is zero, so the only way to effect exposure is with the EC setting. Although this will get covered in the shooting techniques section, it's a simple enough concept. If your test shots are too bright, dial in some negative EC, if they are too dark add some positive.

If you are shooting in full manual mode with no automatic settings, changing EC will have no direct effect on your images, but it will change what you see in your meter so as long as you subsequently adjust your exposure to the new meter zero, you will get the same end result as if you had used EC in an automatic mode.

I cannot give you a generic recommendation for an EC setting that will always work for you. I would suggest starting with zero EC and adjusting as necessary for your situation, with one exception- single color washes. I will discuss this particular situation in the shooting techniques section, but for now if you encounter a scene where the lighting is solidly one color, dial in at least a -1EC setting. Cameras vary greatly, but I find that all of my Nikons seem to work best in normal theater lighting environments with a -1/3 stop EC set in, so if you shoot Nikon that is what I recommend as a starting point. If you aren't sure, err on the side of underexposure. You can do more to save a slightly underexposed digital image in post production than you can an overexposed image.

One other note before we leave the realm of EC; this isn't really exposure compensation, more of a slight tweak, but most newer digital cameras offer some form of highlight priority mode (Active D lighting mode on Nikons). This slightly tilts your exposures to protect highlights in the image. It has more effect on in camera JPEG images than on raw files, but either way you shoot it's worth turning on.

Vibration Reduction / Image Stabilization

Either your lens (more common) or your camera body (less common) can offer a vibration reduction option. In some models this can also be called image stabilization. At the shutter speeds you will usually be using to capture performances, this is better turned off. The only time I would recommend using it is if you are shooting at slower shutter speeds for static subjects. What is a slow shutter speed? Basically if your shutter speed is the inverse of the focal length of your lens or slower, turn your vibration reduction option on, if you are shooting faster, turn it off. In other words, for the standard 18-55mm lens, if you are shooting at 1/60sec or faster, which you should be, turn it off. If you are shooting a longer zoom lens, say a 100-300mm, and you are shooting at less than 1/200th sec you may want to leave it on, but if you notice your shots are slightly out of focus, turn it off and see if it helps. (If you leave VR/IS turned on at speeds where there isn't any vibration to reduce, sometimes the VR system will induce some shake and cause your images to be slightly out of focus)

Shutter Speed

As we talked about in the background information section, higher shutter speeds will be better at freezing motion, but lower shutter speeds will let in more light and work better in darker scenes. Ultimately the amount of shutter speed necessary to reduce motion blur to a level creatively pleasing to you will be a personal choice, but you have to start somewhere. I recommend starting out at 1/200 sec as your initial shutter speed. Unless your performer is doing a very vigorous dance routine this should be fast enough to freeze their motion, although you may see some motion blur on the hands and feet, especially on fast turns. If you really want to completely freeze all motion and you have enough light, 1/500sec should do the trick. If your child is doing a slow monologue you can probably get away with going down to 1/100 or so safely.

One other note to pay attention to is that if you are using a long lens, generally the slowest shutter speed you want to use will be the same as the focal length of your lens (technically the reciprocal, but that's harder to remember) - in other words, if you are using a 100mm lens, shoot at 1/100 sec or faster. For a 200mm lens, 1/200 sec or faster, and so on. If your lens has vibration reduction or image stabilization, like we discussed earlier, turn it off as long as your speeds are above these minimums, turn it on if you need to go slower.

I will leave you with a few examples to give you an idea of the range of shutter speeds. In the first image, I used a 1/100 sec shutter speed, because even though she was moving quickly, it was very dark in the scene. The image is in focus, but if you look at her feet and hands, you can see the blur from them moving during the exposure.

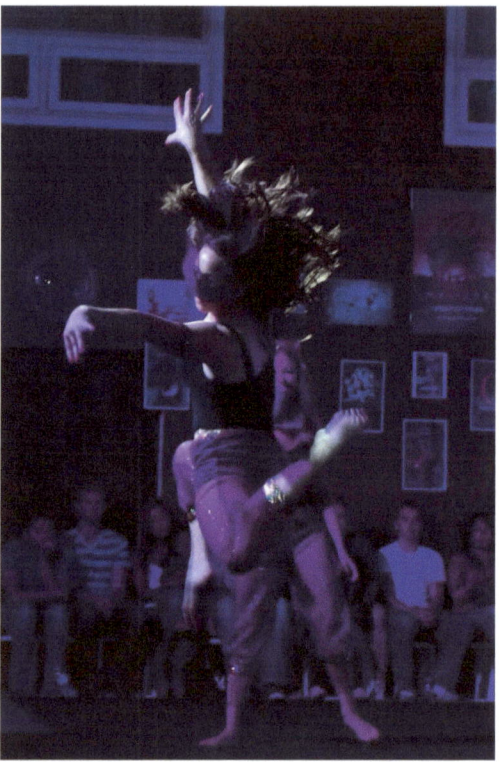

If you have enough light, like I did in this shot, a 1/8000 sec shutter speed is fast enough to freeze almost any motion, including this spinning knife in mid-flight on its' way to a target. (The guy in the back is the instructor for the knife throwing workshop)

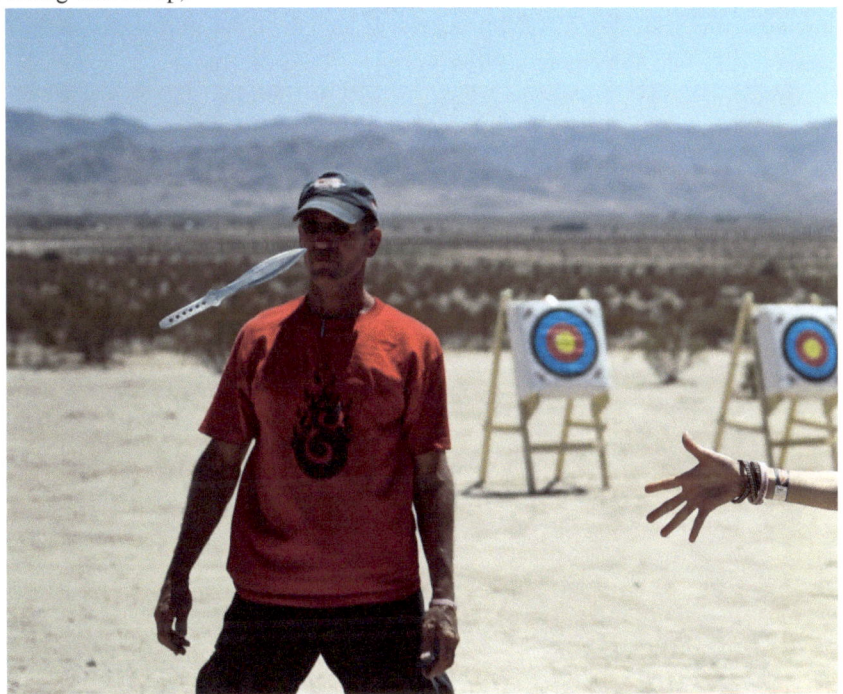

On the other extreme, with long exposures, you can get shots like this one, taken on a tripod with a cable release, the shutter speed was 67 seconds. Not 1/67, but 67, in other words this picture took just over a minute to take. This slow shutter speed allowed me to use a low ISO and high aperture (notice the low noise and wide depth of field) but notice how the lights of the cars on the street just turned into streaks of light?

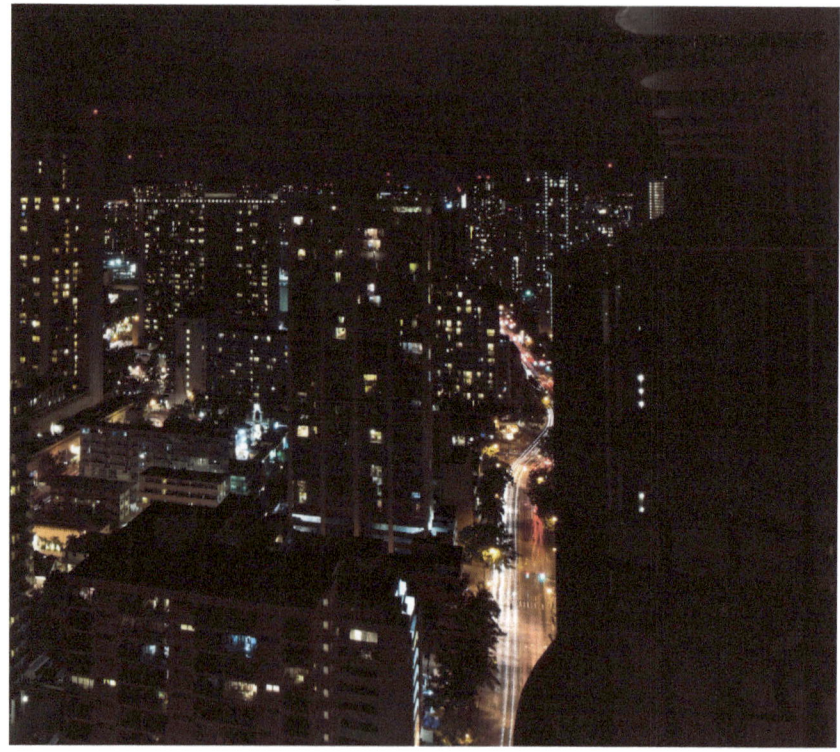

Aperture

If you are shooting in manual as recommended, the final setting you will need to worry about is aperture. If you are shooting in Shutter Speed priority mode, the camera will choose the aperture for you. The one size fits all answer to what aperture to use is: use the widest aperture you can that gives you the depth of field you need to capture what you want. I wish I could tell you what that will be for your situation, but there are too many variables. It will depend on your lens, your camera type, how far away you are from your subject and how much depth of field you need to get everything you want in focus. We covered the way all those variables effect your aperture earlier in the background section, so remember to take them all into account. If you have a smart phone or tablet, there are many applications that will let you calculate the depth of field you will get at a particular distance with your camera/lens/aperture combination.

As a starting point, I would suggest that if you are shooting on a kit lens, start with the widest aperture (smallest number) that your lens has. Unless you are in the front row or shooting with a long telephoto lens, this will probably give you plenty of depth of field to work with. If you have a very fast lens, I suggest stopping it down to around F3.5 as a starting point and opening it up if you find you need more light.

Putting it all together

We've covered a lot of ground so I want to tie it all together before we move on. Unless you made specific exceptions based on your situation as discussed, here is how I suggest you have your camera set up when the curtain goes up and the show begins:

Flash = OFF

LCD Preview = OFF

ISO = Auto mode, capped at your camera's highest useable ISO

Shooting Mode = Manual

White Balance = Flash (unless you know otherwise)

File Type = RAW (at highest bit depth) + JPEG Fine

Metering Mode = Spot

Drive Mode = Single Shot

Focus Mode = Continuous focus, small group of points around the center

Exposure Compensation = - 1/3 (unless you know your camera works best with a different setting)

Vibration Reduction / Image Stabilization = OFF unless using a long zoom lens.

Shutter Speed = 1/200 sec

Aperture = Widest your lens allows or F3.5 if you have a faster lens.

Blinkies = On

Active-D Lighting (highlight priority) = On (medium level if your camera has multiple options for this setting)

Picture Controls: We didn't talk about this earlier, it isn't really a setting, rather it's a collection of presets your camera will apply as it processes images to create its' JPEG versions. If you have one that works for you, stick with it, otherwise go with standard or neutral, or the least processed option your camera offers. These modes won't effect your raw files as they are only applied to camera JPEGs.

There are a few final things that aren't really settings either, but are definitely part of the camera set up process, so I need to cover them. First, make sure you charge your battery before the show, and take along a spare fully charged battery just in case. Second, make sure you have downloaded all the images that were on your camera and spare memory cards, then format your primary and backup memory cards in camera before you leave. You don't want to get to the show and find out that you have an empty battery or a full memory card. Put everything you need in your camera bag the night before and hook your car keys to your bag, that way it's hard to forget it when it's time to head out the door no matter how late you wind up running.

Shooting Techniques

There. Your camera is all set, hopefully I have given you enough of a background that you understand the why behind each of those recommendations, so now let's start the show and get shooting. If you didn't do so earlier, go back and read the EMERGENCY section, concentrating on the parts about what to do when you get to the show and where to sit. I won't take up space and repeat those parts here, so let's assume you are already there, in your seat, and it's showtime.

Adjusting settings on the Fly

Some key things you need to remember before digging into the meat of this section:

When your images are too dark, you need to increase your exposure. You can do this in several ways: Using a higher ISO, Using a slower shutter speed (smaller number), using a wider aperture (smaller number) or using positive exposure compensation.

When your images are too bright, you need to decrease your exposure. You can also do this in several ways: Using a lower ISO, Using a faster shutter speed (larger number), using a smaller aperture (bigger number) or using negative exposure compensation. If you have turned your "blinkies" option on, this will be a quick tool to let you know if your images are too bright. A few blinkies in non critical areas are fine, if large areas of your subject or critical areas are blown out, you will not be able to recover the details afterwards even with raw files.

When shooting digital, it is better to err on the side of under exposing (too dark) versus over exposing (too bright). You have a greater ability to correct for shadows later than for blown out highlights.

Remember that as long as you have any setting in automatic, whether you are in Auto-ISO or shutter/aperture priority, until you have hit a limit on the variable setting, you will not be able to change exposure by changing a single setting, as the camera will automatically adjust the settings it can control to return to what it determines is the proper exposure. The only way you can change exposure with any setting in automatic is by using exposure compensation.

So, with that background in mind, let's start. I will assume you are in the setup I recommended, Manual mode with auto-ISO, starting at around 1/200 sec shutter and F3.5 Aperture (or the widest your lens allows if greater). Hopefully your star is not the first one on the stage at the start of the show, otherwise you will have to do this process very quickly, but here goes:

Once the curtain opens and the lights come up, focus on someone on stage who is in the position your child will be in when they eventually appear (under the spotlight if they have a starring role, or in the background if they are in the chorus) and take a quick test shot. Take a look at this shot on your LCD. First, look at how bright or dark your target subject is. If they are too bright, decrease your exposure, if they are too dark, increase your exposure. (+/- EC) Take another shot and check again, repeat this as necessary until you get the brightness level you want. Once you have this level, take a note of where the exposure meter in your viewfinder is reading. As long as you like the brightness level you see in your test shots, this will be the level you will be looking for throughout the remainder of the show as you shoot.

Once the exposure level is set, take a closer look at your final test image, zoom in if you have to, especially look at the extremities, hands and feet. You are looking for motion blur. If there is some motion blur that you don't want, increase your shutter speed and retest until it's gone. As long as you are seeing close to the same level in your meter that means the camera is doing its' job and changing another setting (ISO if you are set up the way we discussed) to keep the same exposure. If you notice the meter going way off the chart (and the lighting hasn't changed) it means you have reached a limit on your auto setting and won't be able to use a faster shutter speed without getting images that are darker than you want.

Once you have the desired level of motion blur, look around the rest of the frame and see if you have sufficient depth of field. If you do not, you can tighten your aperture, again the camera will compensate for this until it reaches its' limits, so watch your exposure meter.

Once you have all your settings dialed in, stop looking at the images as you are shooting. Shoot as much as you can for the rest of the show without peeking, because each moment you spend looking at the LCD is a moment that you are missing shots as well as the performance. Keep an eye on your meter as you are shooting, as long as it stays close to the reference value you noted while doing your test shots (within a stop) you will be fine. If you really have to, take a quick look back at a few shots between scenes during the set changes. Also, in case you didn't catch this in the Emergency section, I will repeat it here: Unless you are running low on memory card space, never delete images on your camera based on the LCD preview. That small display is not calibrated and does not always give a good representation of what your final image will look like, especially if you are shooting raw. Also, deleting files in camera increases the chance of causing card errors and losing additional images. Save the deleting for later on after the images are on your computer and you are looking at them on a real monitor.

If the meter goes significantly off your standard, this means the lighting conditions have changed. What do you do now? If you feel comfortable you can adjust your exposure compensation without taking your eye off of the viewfinder. This is the best way, because you don't miss anything. If the meter pegs low, you need to increase your exposure. If it pegs high, you need to decrease it. If you don't feel comfortable adjusting without looking, you will need to repeat the test shot sequence as detailed above whenever there is a major lighting change.

If you aren't shooting manual with auto-ISO, or in a priority mode, you will have a little different process. If you are shooting full manual mode, you will be able to adjust any of the three main controls in order to change exposure- ISO, shutter speed, or aperture. If you are in full manual, remember, all the exposure compensation setting will do is move your meter's zero point. In this mode, if you need to reduce exposure I recommend using ISO, because a lower ISO will give you cleaner images. On the other hand, if you need to increase your exposure, I would start with opening aperture then lowering shutter speed as long as you still can get the depth of field and motion freeze you need then raise your ISO as a last resort. Otherwise the test shot process and meter use will be the same as described above. Remember though, if you are in a priority mode, you may not see your exposure meter unless you have EC dialed in. As long as you don't see the exposure meter bar, your camera meter thinks you are in the right ball park, so you will have to judge off the LCD each time there is a significant light change.

If you are reading this far enough in advance, take some time before the show, pull your camera out one evening and play with these settings and practice making adjustments. You may have a separate dial for shutter speed and aperture (they may switch which controls which depending on which mode you are in) or you may have a single dial that needs to be used in conjunction with a button to change the second value. ISO will be a menu option, although on some cameras it can also be accessed via a button/dial combination. Learn which way the dials turn to increase/decrease each setting. The more comfortable you are changing these settings without taking your eyes from the viewfinder, the better your show shooting experience will be.

Finally, you need to be able to find and operate all the important controls on your camera in the dark, because once the house lights go down you probably won't be able to see the labels on your buttons. Practice ahead of time will make your life much easier on show night.

Focusing Technique

If you already know what back button focus is, now is the time to use it, but don't worry if you haven't heard of it before, I will discuss this technique when we get to the professional section. For now I am going to assume you activate your autofocus by pressing your shutter button. Before we start, although I won't go into any sort of technical discussion of camera focus systems, it is important for you to understand a couple of key things.

First, any camera autofocus system requires both a certain minimum amount of light and a certain minimum amount of contrast to function. This means that if it is too dark, your camera will not be able to focus. Even if there is plenty of light, if you are trying to focus on a black costume against a black background, or a white costume against a white background, it will be very difficult for your camera to focus. If your camera's autofocus system is hunting (cycling back and forth without ever locking focus) it means there is not enough light or contrast for the system to function. (If there is plenty of light and contrast and your AF hunts, you need to get your camera/lens checked out by a repair facility)

Second, there are two different types of focus sensors in your camera. You don't have to know which are which, just know that in general the more central the focus point is in the viewfinder, the more accurate it is. Different cameras have different distributions of the types, but all will have the most accurate types clustered at and around the center of the viewfinder. (If you really want to know, the two types of sensors are Cross and Line, the Cross type are the more accurate. You can visit your favorite search engine for more details if you need to know) Most cameras and external flashes also offer some form of focus assist light, if you have this option, keep it turned off for the same reasons I have given for not using your flash. If you are set to continuous focus it will be off by default, at least for Nikon systems. Another great option that some cameras offer is the ability to illuminate the chosen focus points in your viewfinder. If your camera has this option, use it, it will make your life much easier.

Given the constraints of your AF system, there will probably not be enough light in between scenes for your AF system to function, so you will have to wait for the lights to come up. If your star is under the spotlight, you should be able to easily focus on them once their scene begins. The important thing here is to make sure your focus point is entirely covered by your target. If not, you may wind up focusing on something behind them that is also under the focus point. The camera doesn't know which piece of information under the focus point you are trying to capture, it has to guess. Sometimes it will get it right, sometimes it won't. You can tell this is happening if you look at your images and part of them is in perfect focus, just not the part you wanted. Most cameras will offer you an option to view your images with the chosen focus point highlighted, which will allow you to zoom in on the image and see if this is happening to you. If it does, you may have to aim at the center of their chest instead of the face because this will generally be a larger target. If you do focus on the chest, pay attention to the costume color, if it's significantly different in tone from the face, you may have to adjust your exposure compensation because of the effect on your meter. You could also use the focus and recompose technique discussed in the next section.

If your performer is part of a really dark scene, or is on a darker part of the stage outside of the spotlight, you may have a difficult time finding focus. If your lens just continues hunting (focusing back and forth and never locking) you only have a couple of options. First, try to find a point on your subject that has more contrast, If their costume has different color pants and top, the waistline may give you enough contrast to allow your AF system to work, if the costume is a different color from their skin tone the neckline is also another possible target for good contrast. If that doesn't work, you have two or three options left. First, if there is a brighter spot that is roughly the same distance from you as your subject, you focus and recompose. This means you aim at the brighter spot, press your shutter button down halfway to focus, then without letting your finger off the button you move your camera so that your superstar is your target, then press all the way to take the picture. Before you can use this technique; however, you need to switch your AF mode from continuous to single shot, otherwise as you recompose it will attempt to refocus and the trick won't work. Be creative and don't just look on stage, I have successfully used exit signs, lights from backstage in the wings and even once the light from someone's iPhone screen as they were taking a video. It doesn't have to be exact, just close enough to the same focal plane as your target to be within the depth of field range for the aperture you are using. If there is nothing you can use, the second option you have is switching to manual focus. Back in the day that was the only option, and while slower, your eyes can still be better than the best AF systems out there in low light. You can practice this at home, first in a light then in a dark room, before you go to the show just in case you have to do it. The final option is live view, if your camera offers it. This means you are using your rear LCD screen as a viewfinder. I would not use this unless there is no other way, because the light will annoy your fellow audience members, but if you absolutely need the shot I would be remiss not to let you know the option exists. Many cameras offer different AF mode choices in Live View, you will need to consult your manual to see how yours works, and you will also have the manual focus option with a larger, better lit image than the viewfinder, and you may even be able to zoom in and really get a good handle on your manual focus.

That's focusing in a nutshell, just like the previous chapter where I talked about adjusting settings on the fly, the most important thing is to practice as much as possible with your camera and lenses before the show, so you can change modes quickly and easily and have a good feel for how your particular camera, range of focus points and modes work. That's the real beauty of digital cameras, you can take as many practice shots as you want and it doesn't cost anything other than a few moments of your time.

It's all in the Timing!

When it comes to shooting performances, or any other type of action, timing of your shutter is key. If you are used to shooting with a phone or a point and shoot, you know what shutter lag is- that time between you pushing the button and your camera actually taking the picture. DSLRs have much shorter shutter lag than those cameras do, but even though it is minuscule, it is still present, even on the highest end cameras.

Timing is a blend of two factors. The first is physical, you need to get familiar enough with your camera and its' shutter lag to know how many milliseconds before the moment you want to capture that you have to push the shutter button so your camera takes the image right at the instant you are trying to record. I don't mean that you need to pull out a stopwatch and figure out the exact lag time, or look it up online, just that you need to get to the point where you know it instinctively and can hit the button precisely when you need to. For example, let's imagine your dancer is about to make an epic twirling leap across the stage. You see the wind up, you half press the shutter button to lock focus, track them as they step lightly across the stage and leap into the air, then trip the shutter perfectly just an instant before the peak of the arc so you capture the full height of the jump and full expression of your dancer's art. This takes more than just knowing your shutter lag, you also have to know that leap is coming, which brings us to the second part.

The second, and by far the more important skill, is learning when that moment will come so you are ready for it. Experience helps. The more familiar you are with the art form your star will be performing, the easier it will be to anticipate when things are coming. For example, if you have been a dancer your whole life, you can recognize the preparations for a major leap or a particular step even if you have not seen this particular number before. If you haven't practiced the particular art, you can still gain vicarious experience (and bonus points for spending time with and interest in your child and their hobby) by watching them rehearse or practice. This is even better when they are rehearsing for the show you will be shooting. If you watch them practice over and over again, you will know exactly when the big moments are coming. If it doesn't disrupt their concentration you can even practice your shutter timing while they are practicing their part.

Don't despair if you haven't been able to watch a rehearsal and don't have much experience. There are still cues you can use to get ready if you pay attention. If it's a play, there will often be a slow building up of emotion or tension throughout a monologue, you can wait for the tension to burst in a dramatic moment. Plays are a bit harder than musicals or dance numbers. If there is a musical number, you just need to follow the music. Unless your star is performing some sort of avant guard piece to strange atonal music you should be able to hear the music build to key moments. Big moves will usually follow the big beats in the music, or if the music gets slower and softer there may be a good emotional moment coming in the dance. Often as a musical phrase repeats, a certain step will also be repeated, so if you miss it the first time you can be ready to catch it the second or third time. (For some reason three times seems to be the limit for repetition, so don't expect to see something more times than that)

Timing, microseconds, and quite honestly a little bit of luck are what separates good shots from great shots. But luck definitely favors the prepared, so the more you can learn ahead of time about what you will be shooting, the better your shots will be. It also will give you a chance to spend a little more quality time with your child doing something they love. Also, the more you shoot, the better your shots will get as you just get more fluid.

One final note, don't get too discouraged if it seems like you always manage to catch your star with their eyes closed. This probably isn't because you are always timing your shots wrong. Performers, especially solo dancers, tend to go inside themselves when doing complicated maneuvers and have their eyes closed a lot of the time. It probably isn't your camera timing, and there really isn't anything you can do about it.

Dealing With a Single Color Wash

Single color wash lighting, especially when using LED stage lights, may look great on stage to your eye, but it makes your light meter's job incredibly difficult. Red is the worst case, followed by blue and then green. Earlier we covered camera sensor design and how each individual sensor site can only detect a single color of light. Your camera has two green sensors for each red or blue, since green is the most common color in the natural world. Stage lighting; however, doesn't have to conform to reality.

Basically, what happens in a single color wash is that only the sites that see that color realize there is light on the scene. (Conventional lights are a little better because the colors are less pure than LED, but the effect still happens) In other words, if there is only green light, only half your sensor sites detect light, so your camera meter thinks there is about half the light in the scene as there is. If it's red or blue that drops down to around 1/4. I can't prove this other than experience, but I believe red is actually worse than blue since it is the opposite of green on the color wheel for light. This means if you expose according to the meter in a single color wash scenario your shots will all be blown out.

I will discuss how to do a little bit of correction and salvage work on these images in the post processing section later, but what you can do after the fact with a blown out image is very limited. The best way to fix this is in camera. If you see a single color wash, you need to reduce your exposure by at least a full stop over what your meter recommends, For a red or blue wash you may need to reduce even farther. If you have time, I would recommend repeating the test shot sequence we covered at the start of this section, paying careful attention to your blinkies in your test images. Drop your exposure until there are no blown out areas you need detail in (your performers face, costume, etc.)

This image is what happens when you shoot in a single color wash. This exposure was correct according to the meter, but as you can see it is pretty much blown out.

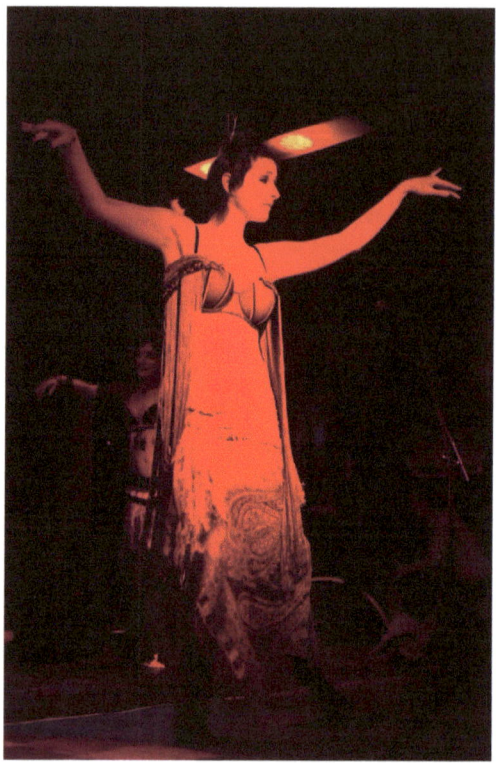

Post Processing

The Show is over, what next?

Now you have all your images, it's time to learn how to make them look their best.

Post Processing Software

If you are only shooting JPEG and don't want to mess with photo editing, you don't actually need any sort of post processing software, although it is still helpful to have some sort of Digital Asset Manager (DAM) software such as iPhoto (if you are a Mac user) to keep your images organized and easily accessible. I will be mostly discussing Mac software in this section, because that is what I use and I am not familiar enough with Windows to advise you on equivalent software packages. Luckily, some of the big names have both Mac and Windows versions. If I don't mention a particular program, that doesn't mean it isn't good, it just means that I don't use it and am not familiar with it, so don't take the little information I present here as all inclusive or the only way to go. I can only speak to what I know, and there are too many options out there for me to know even a significant fraction of them.

Digital Asset Managers are basically the electronic version of a bookshelf full of photo albums. You could accomplish the same thing by setting up your own system of folders and keeping track of which ones your images are in by labeling the folders. What makes these asset managers a better option is that they automate the process, give you the ability to sort your images in various ways, and also allow you to select various ways to display them. While each photo DAM will have its' own unique setup, almost all of them will give you options to rate your photos, add particular images to multiple albums, (without having to duplicate the file and require additional storage space) assign keywords, captions and other meta-data to your images (that you can later use in searches) and even to easily create photo-books, cards and other items to have physically printed. Most will also allow you to do some basic image editing. iPhoto on the Mac is a good example of a basic photo DAM program.

If you are shooting raw and / or you want to do more extensive editing, you will need some level of post processing software. There are many different levels you can choose, depending on your budget and what you want to do. The first step up the ladder would be something along the lines of Aperture (for Mac only) from Apple, or Lightroom (both Mac and Windows) from Adobe. Both are basically DAM programs with extensive editing capabilities built in. If you spend some time online you will see arguments on various photography and editing forums as to which is better and why, ultimately it boils down to which system you like better. I personally use Aperture as my primary program, but for some uses I switch to Lightroom. Either will be able to handle your raw images, provided you have the most recent updates (sometimes it take a while for a new camera's raw format to make it into the wild). Aperture and Lightroom have their own internal raw converters, so you don't need an additional step or program to use these applications with your raw files. Before you can use your raw images in programs that don't have built in raw conversion ability, you will need to process your images in some sort of raw converter. Adobe makes one called Adobe Camera Raw and each individual camera manufacturer makes their own program to convert their camera's images for use. You do not need an external converter if you use Aperture or Lightroom, but you can experiment with them if you like. If you particularly like the JPEG previews your camera comes up with, the easiest way to replicate that effect (other than shooting raw + JPEG, that is) will be to use your camera maker's converter, which should be able to emulate all your camera's settings.

Once you get past the basic programs (and I only mean basic by comparison; both Aperture and Lightroom are very sophisticated programs that offer a lot of editing capability) there are heavy hitters out there, most famously Photoshop. Photoshop used to be prohibitively expensive for most of the general pool of camera users, but they now have monthly cloud subscription plans that are somewhat reasonable if you use the software a lot. Since I do this professionally, I bit the bullet and sprung for photoshop, but don't feel like you have to. There are alternatives out there, Pixelmator and Gimp come to mind, but I have not really used these so I cannot compare and contrast here.

What none of these editors can do is rescue an image that was completely dead on arrival. Even though things an experienced photoshopper can do may seem like magic, if you have blown out the highlights in your shot completely they cannot be saved. If there is too much motion blur or poor focus lock, the image can't be saved. But as long as your initial exposure was in the ballpark and your focus was good you will be surprised at what you can do with your images once learn how to use your editing tools. Getting truly proficient will take time, experimentation, and research on your part, but you can find plenty of tutorials and examples online for whatever software package you choose to use.

When you are doing your editing, you should always make sure your original images are protected, that way you can start from the beginning if you don't like where you end up. Aperture and Lightroom are non-destructive editors. This means that they do not directly edit the original image file, they merely record all the changes you make and apply them prior to displaying or exporting the edited image. You can revert to your original image anytime. Not all editors are non-destructive. If your editor isn't a non-destructive editor, or you aren't sure, always work on a copy of the original image. (Photo shop can be either, depending on how you use it, but unless you are careful it is a destructive editor)

Finally, there are additional add ons called plug-ins that are offered for almost all of the major software packages. Plug ins for specific tasks can save you a lot of time and effort and make your life easier. I will talk a little more about these later in the noise reduction section, because that is where they become important for your performance images. Once you choose your DAM and / or your editing software, you can search online to see what options you have for plug ins that work with your programs of choice.

Most software companies will offer some sort of trial period to let you see if you like that particular package, so, choose your software and let's start playing.

Preparing To Work With Your Images

Before you can work with your images you will need to import them. I will assume you will be working with some sort of DAM program, as discussed in the previous section, and want to organize your images from the start. I will keep this fairly general since I don't know what program you decided to use. If you already have a system in place for organizing your photos, you can either skip this section or read it and see if I can manage to teach you something new or give you a different perspective on how to set things up.

Start your DAM program and plug your memory card into your computer. (You can plug your camera in directly, but it is faster to remove the card from the camera and use either a dedicated slot, if you computer offers one, or a card reader). Once the card is inserted, your DAM should detect it automatically (you may have to set your computer to do this, but most do it by default) and bring you to the import dialogue. You should see a collection of thumbnail icons and have some method of selecting either all or them, or only particular ones you want to import. You should also have the option to do some batch editing on both the images and their meta data as a part of the import process. In case these terms are unfamiliar to you- batch editing simply means doing the same thing to multiple files at the same time. Meta Data is data (besides the image itself) that is attached to your image file. Some of it is fixed (the file will contain meta data that records camera information, settings and time of capture) and some you can change, like the image title, caption, copyright information, location data, and keywords. It is much simpler to edit this during import than later. You can also use presets to make adjustments to the image itself during import. You will also be able to choose where to import your files to.

Import Location: Your system will be unique to you, I group my images using a system of folders. Professionally I create a folder for each client, then within that a subfolder for each year, then within that folder an album for each shoot/ show. Personally, I start with the year as the largest folder, and within that I have categories like: travel, birthdays, shows, etc. Each of those has its' own folder and I make each set of images an album. There are probably as many file organization systems as there are photographers, it may take some trial and error but eventually you will find one that works for you.

Image Name: I prefer to give the images a name that will be more helpful than the generic one the camera spits out. I try to work the date and something descriptive of the shoot into the name, then end with a sequential number. (The import process will automatically add the sequential numbers) For example, if I shot a dance recital for a studio on June 6th, 2014, the file names would look like this: 2014June06ABCstudio_1, 2014June06ABCstudio_2, etc. That way even if I export them later out of my folder system, I still know what they are without having to open them and check. It also makes it easier for clients to tell me which particular images they are asking for.

Title/Caption/Copyright/Location: I generally leave the title blank, I put anything I need to remember about the shoot in the caption field, I always put my own name and / or my studio name in the copyright line, and fill out the location data. You can decide what you want to use, but it's easier to add it now than later.

Keywords: Keywords are amazing. You can use whatever you want, and they will give you a lot of flexibility later on to search your images. You can use generic keywords like: Dance, Theater, Show, or anything you want. You can also add specifics like your superstar's name, the name of the show, whatever you want.

Once you have all your import settings ready, you click to start the import, then have a glass of wine or beer and let the computer get the job done. The meta data and key wording may seem like a lot of work, but it's worth it. This is where your DAM program really shines and shows why it is better than just tossing all your files straight from your card onto your hard drive. Later on, you can search using all those keywords you put in, through all your photos. Let's say you want to put together a graduation slideshow of all your star's performances over the years for a graduation party. You can ask your DAM to show you all images with the keywords (for example) "name of your star," "dance" and "recital," and in a second you will be able to scroll through every dance recital shot of your dancer you have on file. Keywording is incredibly powerful once you get it set up. Minutes spent in key wording during upload can save hours sorting through images later trying to find one you want.

Ok- your images just finished importing. The program will probably ask you if you want to keep or delete the images and whether to eject the card. I recommend you keep the images on your card, because you aren't done yet. These are important images, memories of your child you want to treasure. Now you have two copies- one on your computer and one on your memory card. Before you delete the images on your card, or do anything else, I suggest running a backup using whatever backup software you use, so you will have multiple copies of your images before you delete them off your card. (Professional photographers usually keep multiple backups of their images and keep at least one backup copy off site- either in the cloud or at an alternate location just in case their studio burns down and destroys all their computers, but it's up to you if you need that level of backup security)

Once your images are imported and backed up, you can put your card back into your camera and reformat it so you are ready for your next shoot. It is always better to reformat your card in the camera you will be using it in, because each camera may have its' own slightly peculiar format. Just deleting the images on the computer and replacing the card without reformatting opens you up to more potential for card problems. Which brings us to the next topic.

OH NO — MY CARD IS BAD! if you have any issues with your card, maybe something is corrupted and you cannot import the images onto your computer-, or maybe your camera won't record anymore and gives you a card error alert signal, do not despair yet. Take that card out and set it aside, do not reformat it or do anything to it. There is a special type of software out there called data recovery software. Major memory card manufacturers each make their own version and you may be able to get a free copy with purchase of their cards. Sandisk and Lexar both offer this. (which is one reason those cards have such a great rep with pros). I have personally used Lexar's Image Recovery software and it's saved my rear after a card was "corrupted" by my young superstar playing with my camera. Not only did the software recover those images, it also recovered images from past shoots even after multiple formats of the card. Hopefully you'll never need recovery software, but if you do, it's nice to know it exists and can sometimes work miracles.

One final note for those of you working with raw images for the first time- when you import them and view them in your image editor, don't be surprised if they look horrible. This is normal. We'll talk about that more in the next section.

Basic Raw Image Work

I mentioned this at the end of the last section, but it is important so I will start off with it here. If you are used to working with only JPEG images, the first time you see your imported raw images on your screen prepare for a shock, they will probably look horrible. Remember, the JPEG image you see on the back of your camera is a processed, finished image. (Technically it's a preview version of one, but close enough) The raw image you see on your computer is (unless you applied a preset at import) the unprocessed, undeveloped image. The result is that it starts flat and yucky looking. The advantage is that you get to develop it to your own tastes instead of the camera's. Some programs, like Aperture, for example, initially (unless you direct it not to) use the camera's embedded jpeg preview (the same one you saw on your LCD) as a preview, so the image will look finished until you click on it and the raw loads. This shift can be confusing to watch, as the pretty finished JPEG preview is replaced by the flat raw version, but you get used to it. If you like the camera JPEG versions most of the time, you can either use your camera company's raw converter software (which should, in theory, be able to emulate the conversion settings you camera would use) or shoot in RAW + JPEG mode, so you can use the JPEG versions you like but still have the raw if you need to do more extensive corrections. You may also be able to find presets online that you can download and import into your DAM to mimic your camera's conversions.

So what corrections will you need to do? The most important is noise reduction, but before that you may want to do a few things. The first thing I do is go through and rate my images, from "this one is destined for my portfolio," down to "this one isn't salvageable and just needs to get deleted." That way I don't waste my time working on images that aren't going to be good no matter how much I do to them. Once I know which images I am going to work on, I check the basic settings that apply to all the images. I will correct the white balance if necessary, add a bit of sharpness and make any other global corrections I see that apply to most or all of the image set. Then I will go through and crop each image that needs it. After that I will go through and look at the images to find groups of similar images (lighting, costume, etc). I will edit the first of each group to a setup I like, adjusting exposure, shadows, highlights, etc. This would turn into an encyclopedia if I tried to describe each adjustment, your best bet is to get either a book or online tutorial for your particular software package. Once I get the first image in each group set so it looks like I want it to, I will batch apply the same corrections to all the images in that group, then check through them and make any minor tweaks I need to.

If I really need extra horsepower for a particular image I will either use a plug in within my DAM or I will open the image in photo shop for more extensive work. This is more frequent in my portrait shoots, I don't often have to go this far with my performance shots, unless I am specifically prepping a single image for a contest or for my portfolio.

My last step is noise reduction, which is important enough to rate its' own section.

Noise Reduction

The biggest post production task you will face with most of your performance photography is noise reduction. If you are using Lightroom you are in luck because LR has a pretty awesome noise reduction capability built into it. Aperture has a noise reduction adjustment as well, but it doesn't work nearly as well (at least in the current versions). To get around this I use several plug ins, but my favorite by far is NoiseWare. Others I use are Topaz Denoise and Nik Dfine. All three work really well, the main reason I prefer the NoiseWare plug in is that is allows me to batch process multiple images while the other two require me to work on a single image at a time.

There is a lot to noise removal and the best technique for each different type of noise, the two main types being luminance and chrominance noise. You can spend a lot of time online or in books learning more detail than you ever wanted to know if you really want to dive deep, but for our purposes you really just need to know how to do the job, if you want to know more feel free to research and learn on your own. The most important thing I can tell you before I explain my workflow for noise reduction is that you only want to use the least amount of noise reduction you need to get your images down to an acceptable level of noise. If you overdo noise reduction your images will take on a weird, almost plastic-doll look and will just not look real. Overdoing the noise reduction can also destroy detail.

Here is an image straight out of the camera. This was shot at ISO 12,800, the highest native ISO on my D4. The noise isn't too bad, but if you look, especially at the background, you can see it.

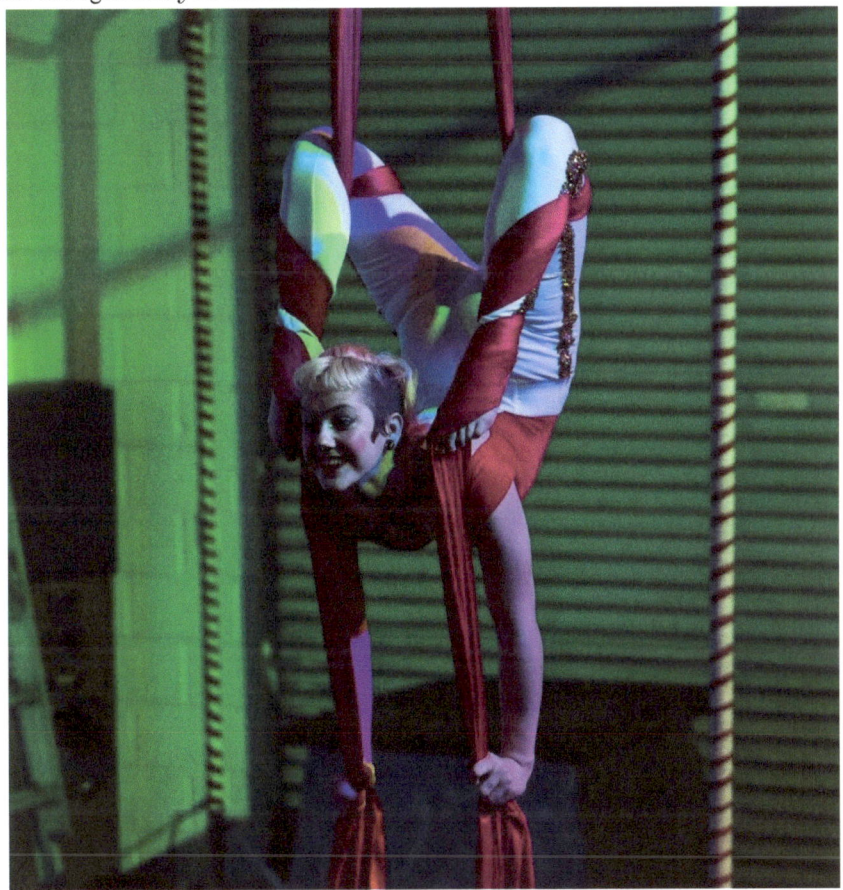

Here is the same image after processing with the NoiseWare plug-in. You can see it wiped out most of the noise, but there is a little corresponding loss of detail.

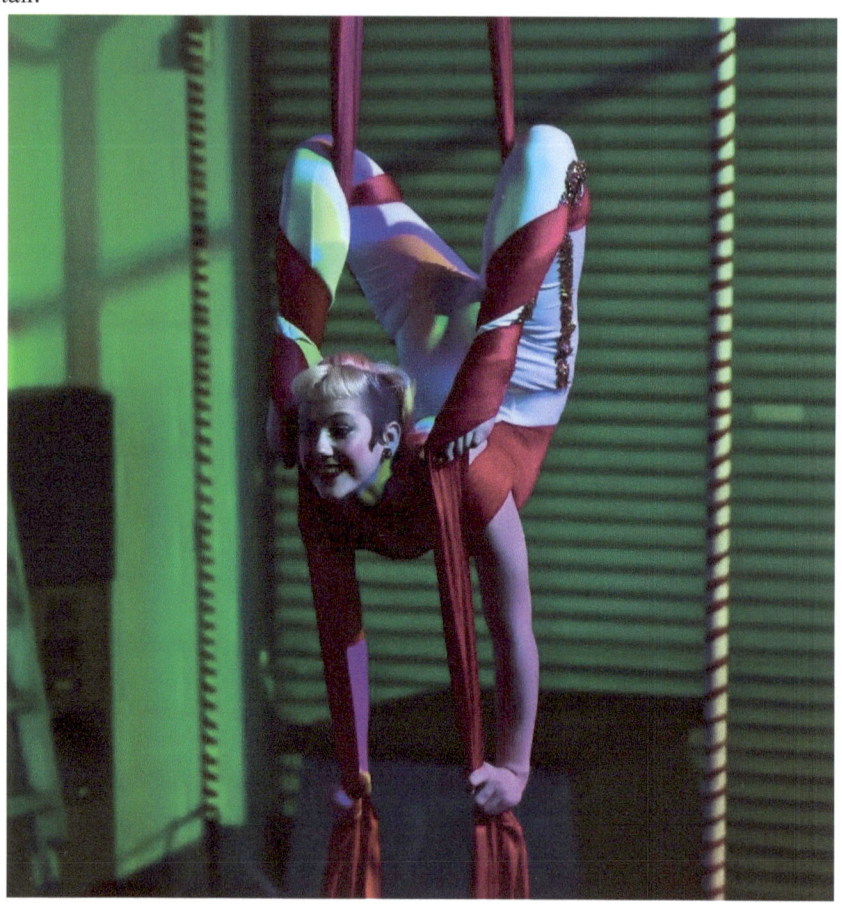

I am by no means an expert on noise reduction, but I have gotten to a pretty good level of familiarity with my tools, so here is what I do. Common editing wisdom says to do noise reduction first, before any other edits. If I was using LR and removing noise in the raw file, I would do that, but Aperture and my noise reduction plugins don't work that way, when using a plugin aperture creates a second version of the file in a TIFF format with the plug in action applied, so I save this step for last in my workflow. First I do all my image rating and selection, then perform all my cropping and other edits. When that is done, I group all the edited shots by noise levels. Basically this boils down to groups of shots taken in similar lighting conditions at similar camera settings throughout the performances. Once I have the images grouped by noise level, I batch edit each group using the NoiseWare plug in with the lowest possible reduction settings that get me to an acceptable level of noise. (some groups may need no reduction at all) When the edit is done I go back through the group and make sure each one worked correctly and nothing strange happened, then I move on to the next group. If any images didn't work out right with the batch settings I go through and individually edit them, either with Noiseware again or with one of the other plug ins, as each one works slightly differently. The Nik plug ins are nice for fine tuning because if you need it you can selectively apply NR to certain parts of your image via something the software calls "control points." It's more labor intensive but very controllable when you need it.

Once they are all done, you're ready to post, share and enjoy.

Single Color Wash

One final topic I will cover in the post production section is the dreaded single color LED wash. We covered this in the shooting techniques section, so hopefully you were able to adjust your exposure down enough that you have useable shots. If they still look blown out, you can correct them to some extent in your editing flow, so if you have an otherwise good shot that was blown out by a single color wash, you can at least try a few of these techniques before giving up on it.

The first and simplest is to drop the exposure down even further in post. You can also try using a highlight recovery adjustment if you have one in your editing suite. If these simple adjustments don't do the trick you can also try dropping down the overall saturation or vibrance in the image. The final "easy" edit to save a single color wash shot is to turn it into a black and white version, as this will sometimes render an otherwise blown out shot into something useable. If these techniques don't work, there is one more option if you really want to go the extra mile.

You may recall the image I used earlier to illustrate the red wash and its' consequences:

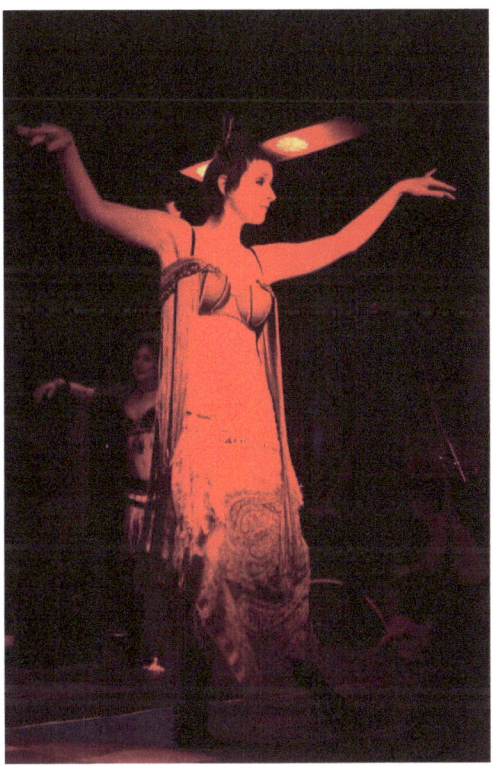

Here is the best save I could get for this image by reducing exposure, dropping the overall saturation and vibrance and tweaking the contrast, shadows and balance a little bit. Still not great but better.

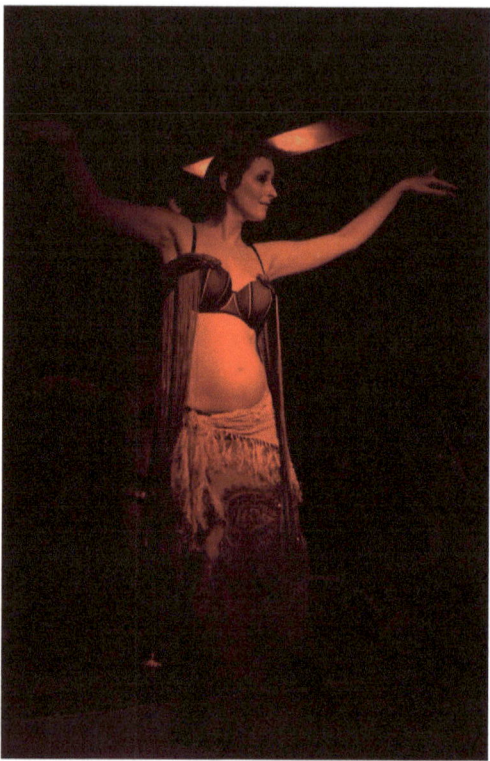

The same image converted to black and white and tweaked a little bit.

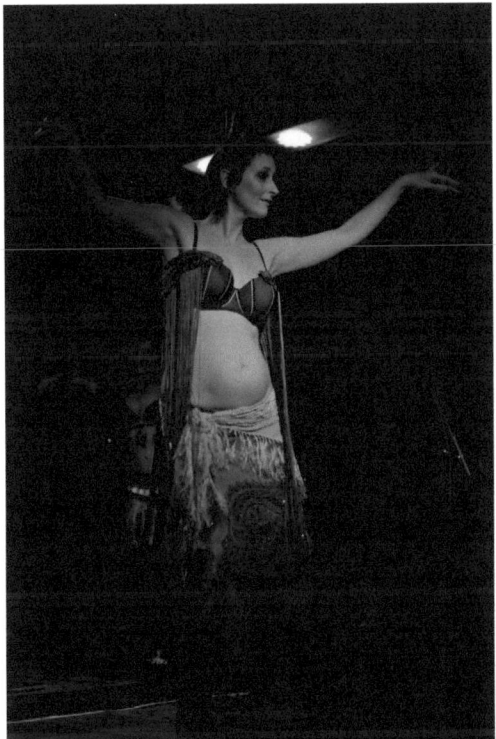

Your final option is to put the image into a heavy duty editor like photoshop, break down the image to its' component color channels, and then selectively lower the channel corresponding to the wash color while increasing the other channels. This is something new I am experimenting with and I haven't gotten it down to a science yet, if I figure it out I will update it in a future edition. If you are already a high level photo shop user you may be able to do this better than me already, but if not it may be worth playing with if you really want to salvage an image.

133

That is the last thing I think we need to over for post processing, time to start wrapping things up. I know I didn't really cover post processing in a lot of detail, and I apologize for that. I wish I could give you specific formulas, and tell you exactly which settings you need to tweak by precisely how much in order to make your images shine. Believe me, if I would, I could, but there is so much variation out there that I can't. Although the batch editing process is great, each different set of lighting conditions and each image set you have will require different adjustments and techniques to make them look their best. It's a lifelong study and there are no "one size fits all" answers. I have included a few links at the end to give you places to start looking and learning more.

Pro Gear and Techniques

The Next Level

What Do the Pros know/have that you may not?

Professional Level Gear and Techniques

Now that you know the basics, let's talk about what the professionals have that you may not and what they do that you may not have tried yet. These factors boil down to three main areas: high end camera bodies, professional lenses, and shooting techniques. Some of this information will be a rehash and expansion of what we have already covered in the basic chapters on equipment, but the shooting techniques section will have some things that you can use regardless of your equipment budget.

Professional Lenses (aka Fast Glass)

Professional lenses are separated from their consumer level counterparts by more than just price, weight and build quality. The two main advantages that come with high end lenses for our purposes are better optics and wider apertures. The first things you will notice after you get over the sticker shock and pick up a professional lens is that it will be larger and heavier than a similar focal length lens in the consumer grades. It will generally also have a larger front element, which lets in more light. Professional primes will open up to F1.4 or even farther, zooms will open to F2.8, at least in the focal lengths you will likely be using for shooting performances. Sigma has just come out with a DX specific F1.8 zoom that claims to put DX performance on par exposure wise with a full frame F2.8 zoom, but I have not tested this yet. Lens technology continues to improve and if this lens is a success then other manufacturers will soon follow suit.

Professional lenses will generally offer faster and quieter autofocus motors, vibration reductions options for some focal lengths and models, and better coatings on the lens elements. All of these differences add up to significantly improved performance, especially in the low light conditions you will find yourself in so often during shows.

If you can afford pro glass and don't mind carrying the extra weight, go for it. If you can't, it isn't the end of the world. If you are only shooting an occasional show, once or twice a year, and don't need the extra lens performance on a routine basis, you can rent a lens to use for the show, or even to test out and see if you think it's worth buying. Your local camera store may offer rental options, if not there are a few rental houses you can find online that will ship your rental to you. I will include a few links in the resources section at the end of the book.

If you do rent gear; however, be sure to put it on your camera, test it out, and get used to it before you bring it to the show.

Professional Cameras

Unless you are in very demanding low light conditions, you will be able to get quality images from a basic level DSLR and kit lens combo. Unless your child is older and performing in the local nightclub scene, you will be fine with whatever DLSR and lens combo you currently have in all but the moodiest, darkest scenes. So if a $500 camera can get the images you need, what is the point of paying $6000 for a professional camera body?

I already covered the difference between full and crop frame sensors. Beyond this, the higher end camera bodies will generally offer better high ISO performance, faster shooting speeds, less shutter lag and faster autofocus systems with more focus points and options. They will also generally offer a more extensive library of metering references and lots of other bells and whistles in addition to better ergonomics. A camera like the D4, for example, is designed to operate in low light environments and even offers backlit buttons that you can turn on just in case you need to find that one control you don't use all that often in the dark.

If don't need all the performance of a professional body in your daily shooting, I don't recommend going out and buying one just to shoot one or two shows a year. If you need it only occasionally, renting will be a much better option. Even more important than lenses; however, if you are renting a new camera body, give yourself a lot of time before your show to get used to it and find all the controls and settings you will need to use. Also, make sure you have the right memory cards for the rented body, as not all cameras use the same cards.

Pro Shooting Techniques

Shooting Techniques

Gear is important. A talented photographer can make a great image with any camera and lens, but having the right tools for the job does help. A formula one driver is a better driver than me even if they are driving a cheap 4 cylinder rental car, but they won't win a race unless they have a competitive car. That being said, just like I couldn't hop into a formula one race car and fly around the track at top speed without getting into a wreck, don't expect to get incredible shots just because you rented or purchased a professional lens and camera. In fact, if your technique is poor, pro gear may even make your shots worse because it can be less forgiving of small errors. The best example I can provide of this is the Nikon D800. As of this writing, it is the highest resolution DSLR on the market, approaching the image quality and resolution of a medium format system. Lots of people who use this camera for the first time find their images are blurry and out of focus. Mostly it isn't the camera, it's the shooter. With good technique the D800 and a sharp lens are capable of creating amazing images, but if you are even slightly out of focus or are shooting at a low shutter speed with any camera shake at all, the high level of resolution the camera provides makes these small errors glaringly obvious. In a lower resolution camera, you would have never noticed the slight blur that is obvious when looking at a 100% zoom of a 36MP image. Some people think you can only shoot sharp images with the D800 on a tripod, which is true if they try to use the 1/60 or 1/80 second shots they were used to, but at faster shutter speeds that eliminate motion blur, it's tack sharp. Until they learn how to shoot with it though, many D800 users (myself included) suffered some initial disappointment when the camera's incredible capabilities revealed our own shortcomings. I chose to use it as an opportunity to learn to shoot to the capabilities of my gear, a challenge not a setback, and I suggest you do the same if you find yourself able to use higher level gear. Just don't be surprised by the learning curve and definitely take any new gear (regardless of how fancy it is) you plan to use out for a test run or two before you use it on any important occasion.

The newest, shiniest tech is always awesome, and having better tools does open up the range of options of available to you, but always remember that it is the photographer that makes the picture, not the camera. In fact, one of the worst "compliments," a photographer gets all to frequently is, "wow, your camera really takes great pictures….." It makes us want to scream a little. So, other than gear, there are a few tricks and techniques that the pros use that can help set your images apart from the rest. Better technique will give you the greatest improvement in your shooting. Every photographer has their own distinct shooting style and their own bag of go to tricks they have developed over time. As you practice you will find some of your own, but I am going to share a few of the more common and easily adoptable things that I have found very helpful in my own development.

Back Button Focus

One of the most useful techniques I have learned is Back Button Focus. By default your camera will activate your autofocus system whenever you press the shutter button halfway down and you will have to wait for the focus before firing the shutter. Back button focus changes this behavior and will change the way you shoot. Like the name suggests, you are disconnecting the autofocus system from your shutter button entirely and setting a button on the rear of your camera as the AF activation button. Nikon professional bodies already have a dedicated button for this, helpfully labelled "AF-ON," right about where your thumb falls on the camera rear when held in the horizontal position. Some, like the D4, also have a second button in the same relative location for vertical shooting. On lower end Nikons without dedicated AF-ON buttons there is still a button that can be reprogrammed via menus to function as an AF-On button. If you are not a Nikon shooter, a quick search on google will tell you what the equivalent buttons are for your particular camera. Regardless of your camera model, you will have to consult your manual on how properly set your camera up to use only this rear button for focus control.

Why would you want to do this? Quite simply it gives you more control over your camera and a better chance of getting a shot in a difficult situation. I will discuss pre-focusing in the next chapter, as there are multiple ways to do it, but the easiest way is to use back button focus. I originally learned about back button focus when I was researching ways to improve my sports photography. With our default setup, your AF will activate whenever you press the shutter button halfway down; to continually focus on something you have to keep the shutter button half pressed, and there is no way to keep your camera from attempting to focus before each shot. There is also no way to focus and recompose. Back button focus gives you additional control without having to switch your camera to either single shot AF or manual focus. Assuming you are set up for continuous focus mode, as long as you hold the AF-On button down your AF will track whatever is in your designated focus point. You can click the shutter at any point. If something happens and you want the autofocus to deactivate, you take your finger off the button and your focus stays where it was, even if you move the camera and continue to click the shutter button. Why is useful? If no one is onstage but your child and the light is great, it won't make any difference. But what happens if it is a big dance number with the whole cast on stage, and other cast members are continually moving back and forth in front of your child? Using the traditional setup, anytime someone passed between your lens and your child, the autofocus could try to focus on them instead of your intended subject. How does back button focus keep this from happening? During a break in the crowd when you get a good view of your child, you focus using the back button then release it. Now, as long as your child stays in that spot, no matter how many people dance in front of them, they will stay in focus. It also helps when another parent in the row in front of you sticks their camera right in between you and your child. (Note- if you can imagine how annoying that will be to you, try to avoid doing it to any other parents behind you who are also trying to get pictures or just see their kids) If the lighting suddenly dims in the middle of a number or monologue, release the button and you will keep the focus you had even thought the light is now too dim for your AF system to focus. If you were using the normal setting and your AF system tried to refocus and failed, you would not be able to keep shooting.

Just like anything else, using this technique will take practice, but once you have used it for a bit you may find that you like it and start using it as your default method. Once you get over the initial learning curve and get used to the new habit of pressing the back button to focus the camera, most people, myself included, realize how much better shooting this way is. The only downside I have found to using back button focus is that if you are going to hand your camera to someone else to take a picture (so you can be in it) you need to remember to set your AF activation back to the shutter button, because I have found that even if you explain the setup quickly to them, you are likely to get back a blurry image because it isn't how they are used to cameras working. On higher level Nikon bodies you can set this up as part of a custom setting menu which will let you switch from regular to back button focus quickly and easily before handing off your camera. If someone else regularly uses your camera, it's a pretty quick and easy thing to teach them to use the back button as well.

Pre-Focusing

This trick is incredibly easy if you use back button focus. It is useful if the lighting will be either very dark or rapidly changing during a scene, or some other issue like a lack of contrast between costuming and background makes focusing on your subject difficult; however, you can only pre-focus if your scenario meets several key requirements. First, the action that you want to photograph has to occur in a single, well defined location. An example of this would be a singer who you know will come out and do a solo at a pre-placed microphone on stage, or you know that your Juliette will be on the balcony to be wooed by her Romeo. Second, you have to know ahead of time when and where the action will take place and you have to realize ahead of time that you will need to use pre-focusing. Finally, you have to have an opportunity just before the scene in which the area the action will take place is visible and lighted well enough for you to focus on it.

I will use the balcony scene from Romeo and Juliette to describe how to use back button focus, assuming your subject will be Juliette. You know that the lighting they are going to use for this scene will be very dim and Juliette's costume is similar in color to the stage setting. Since we discussed earlier how AF works, you know this will make things difficult for your camera to focus on Juliette once the scene starts. During the scene change you notice the lights that are up for the stagehands are pretty bright, so once the balcony is place you aim your camera at the railing, activate your back button focus, get a good focus on the balcony railing then take your hand off the AF-ON button. The lights go dim. Juliette comes to the balcony and starts to pine for her Romeo. You raise your camera, which is already focused on where you knew Juliette would be, and start shooting, never having changed your focus.

If you have your AF system tied to your shutter button, this won't work, because the first time you try to take a shot, the camera will try to re-focus and if it cannot then you will lose the shot. If you have decided that back button focus isn't for you; don't worry, you can still use pre-focusing, it just takes more work. You would take all the same steps as above, but once you made your initial focus on the balcony during the scene change, you would then turn your autofocus completely off - i.e. Switch your camera/lens to manual focus. This works just as well, but you have to remember to turn your AF system back on when you want to shoot anything else. Using back button focus the AF system is still there the instant you need it again. Some cameras also have a function called auto-focus lock, which would sound like something you could use to make this trick work, but for most cameras that lock only lasts for one shot and then the AF activation reverts to normal operation on subsequent shots. That function is only designed to let you focus and recompose one shot at a time.

One other potential pitfall with pre-focusing is depth of field. If you are shooting with fast glass wide open, especially 1.2/1.4/1.8 primes, and possibly the 2.8 zooms depending on how close you are to the action, you may pre-focus on the balcony only to find that you did not have sufficient depth of field for Juliette to also be in focus. If you are close and wide open, you may also want to stop your lens down a few clicks just to be safe.

Low lit, hard to focus situations are not the only use for this technique. It is also helpful if you are shooting fast action and have a slow autofocus system with your given camera/lens combo. If this is the case and you know a piece of fast action will occur at a given spot, you can pre-focus on where you know the action will happen and be ready to go without an AF delay when it does. Maybe your child is a dancer, and you know their entrance will be a fast, wild leap from behind a piece of scenery at a certain point in a song. Before the key moment in the music comes up you pre-focus on the set piece your child will come from, and then the second they leap out you click the shutter and get the shot that everyone else missed because their cameras couldn't focus quickly enough.

That's pre-focusing. Like the next techniques, I will describe it isn't something you will be able to use all the time, but it's a nice trick to have up your sleeve in case you come across a situation where you can use it. If your performer plays sports, you may find this trick useful there too.

Two Eyed Shooting

Another technique you might not be familiar with is shooting with both eyes open. Your view through the viewfinder will be constrained, especially if you are using a long lens. This means that if you close one eye and use the other to look through the viewfinder, you will only be able to see a very small portion of what is happening on the stage. If you are only following your child around, this may not be a big problem for you, but if you need to be aware of what is going on elsewhere on stage, it will be. Maybe you have multiple children in the same show, or you know your child is about to come out on stage but aren't sure where they will enter from and want to be ready to go, or some part of the action elsewhere will cause a reaction from your star that you want to be ready for. If any of these situations fits or you just want to try something new, you might want to experiment with keeping both eyes open.

Unless you have a special custom model, your camera is set up to be held with your right hand operating the main controls, while your left hand operates the lens and helps support the camera. If you are shooting with one eye it doesn't matter which eye you use, but the design of the camera makes it easier to shoot with both eyes open if you use your right eye on the viewfinder and your left eye for the rest of the world. If I try to reverse that I find that my own hands and arms get in the way.

Shooting with two eyes open can be disorienting at first, so practice it before you try it during a critical scene. It takes some time to get used to seeing the same view differently through either eye, the closest thing I can think of is watching a picture in picture TV display. You always see both shows, but you can really only focus on one at any given time. The trick lies in being able to scan the whole picture with your free eye while balancing the picture through your viewfinder with enough attention to control where your focus points are falling and your framing. It will be difficult at first, and you may find that you can only keep it up for short periods of time before the visual chaos gives you a headache. Don't push it, but if you keep practicing you will get the hang of it and probably find that it is another useful tool to have in your kit.

I don't use it all the time, if I am shooting a single subject that is onstage for a solo I will use one eye, because I am naturally left eye dominant and prefer to have my left eye to the viewfinder if I have the option. But if I am shooting a large group and don't know what's coming and when, I shoot two eyed and swing the camera around as I need to which lets me catch more of the action and get shots I would not have known were there if I was only seeing a small slice of the stage.

Take advantage of Rehearsals

The single most effective thing you can do to get better images of your child's performance is to find a way to shoot a full dress rehearsal instead of an actual performance. Once you have an audience in place you are limited as a photographer. You can't move around to get the best angles and you also have to worry about making noise and bothering the rest of the audience. You can still get great shots, but it's more difficult. A rehearsal is a different animal. There is no audience. As long as you don't interfere with the director or the performers, you are free to move about the house, possibly even to go onstage (out of the actors way) or even backstage to get angles you would not be able to get during the live show. You don't have to worry about the noise from your shutter disturbing the patrons, so if you want to and have a large enough card you can put the shutter on continuous high speed and machine gun away. (I still don't recommend that particular technique, I'm just saying you could) There is also a chance that you will get to see the same scene a couple of times as they run through it and have more than one chance at the shot.

That last statement leads to the second part of this- if you can make it to more than one rehearsal, do it. That way if you miss a shot at the first rehearsal, you will know it is coming for the next and be ready to catch it. You will get to see the lighting and know in advance what settings you will need for a particular scene instead of having to figure it out on the fly. Also, if you are the official photographer for the show, they may be willing to stop mid scene and / or redo certain pieces in order for you to get great shots.

Even if you can't shoot the rehearsal, just watching one will give you a better idea of what to expect and when, which will help you get better shots on performance night. If you can't make a rehearsal, at least watch your child practicing their routine or scene at home, that way you will have at least some idea of what to look for.

Finally, since this book is aimed at the parent taking pictures of your child, shooting the rehearsal lets you get all the images for you to enjoy and share, but it also lets you actually watch the show on opening night without a camera in front of your face and enjoy supporting your child. Trust me, you will both appreciate that. Shooting or watching a rehearsal isn't always an option, but if it is you should always take it.

Panning

Back when we discussed shutter speeds, I briefly mentioned the concept of creating/freezing motion blur through panning, so what is it and how do you do it? Simply put, panning is moving the camera during the exposure. This really isn't an option if you are shooting at high shutter speeds, but it can let you use slower shutter speeds and get some creative results. If you have ever seen an image of a race car, motorcycle, horse, runner, or other moving subject where the subject is in sharp focus but the background is blurred, you have seen panning. Basically, you use a slower shutter speed that would normally show motion blur with a static camera, but you move the camera in sync with the moving subject. This keeps your subject in focus but blurs the background to give a strong sense of movement

This isn't an easy technique and definitely takes a little bit (ok, a lot) of practice to do well, but once you get the hang of it you can get some great images. For performances it would mostly be useful for long solo runs and leaps across the stage, and would only be effective if there was something in the background. If it's a soloist against a blank single color backdrop, panning won't get you that background blur (it will, it just won't matter because it's too uniform) but it will let you use longer shutter speeds, which is always a good option to have.

This really isn't a technique you will use often in theater shooting, but if you want to practice panning, the easiest way to do it is to set yourself up near a busy street or bike path, set your shutter speed to around 1/60th of a second or so, depending on how fast your targets will be moving, and practice. Start tracking the subject with your camera before you hit the shutter, moving with them to keep them centered in your focal point, trip the shutter, and continue your motion. Follow through a little bit after the image, if your subject is still centered in your viewfinder when it re-activates after the shutter trips, you probably got a good shot. Take a look and see how it came out. Longer shutter speeds will allow more background blur but you will have to track the target longer.

Wrap Up

You've reached the end!

Whew. That was quite a journey, but hopefully you learned something and have some ideas to test out that will help you to capture awesome images of your children next time they are on stage. A lot of these same lessons and techniques will also apply to other areas of your photographic life as well. Maybe you want to shoot a candle lit holiday party, or some other occasion where the lights are less bright than you would like. Maybe it's a soccer game or some other fast moving event. Whatever the situation, when you have to shoot fast in low light, you will find a lot of the same techniques and ideas will help.

Finally, I will leave you with one more piece of advice. I have alluded to it throughout the book, but it's important enough that I think I want to mention it one more time on the way out the door. Don't forget to occasionally put the camera down and experience what your child is doing first hand. Capture the memories in your mind, but be fully present for your child. They will appreciate it, and so will you. It's all right to occasionally leave the picture taking to someone else.

More from me.

If you liked this book and want to keep up with what I am doing and follow my journey as a photographer, here is how you can find me:

My portfolio and main online site: http://www.happydragonphoto.com

My blog: http://happydragonphoto.blogspot.com

Those two sites will also link you with my presence on various other social media platforms: Facebook, Google +, Twitter, and anything else that might spring into existence between my writing this and your reading it.

Finally, if you have any comments, questions, feedback or other suggestions regarding the contents of this book, please feel free to contact me at bookfeedback@happydragonphoto.com and I will revise, explain or update as I can.

Thanks for reading and I hope your pictures turn out great!

Links for further study:

One of the best performance shooters out there: Todd Owyeng - www.ishootshows.com

Great resource for online training on everything: www.lynda.com

More Learning: phlearn.com

Photoshop User Forum: forum.photoshopuser.com

Camera and Lens Rental Options:

Borrowlenses.com

Your local camera store

Software:

Topaz Plug Ins: topazlabs.com

Nik Plug Ins: google.com/nikcollection/

NoiseWare: imagenomic.com/nw.aspx

Manuals:

Nikon: support.nikonusa.com

Canon: usa.canon.com/cusa/support/consumer

Front Matter

Shoot Your Child's Show Like a Pro

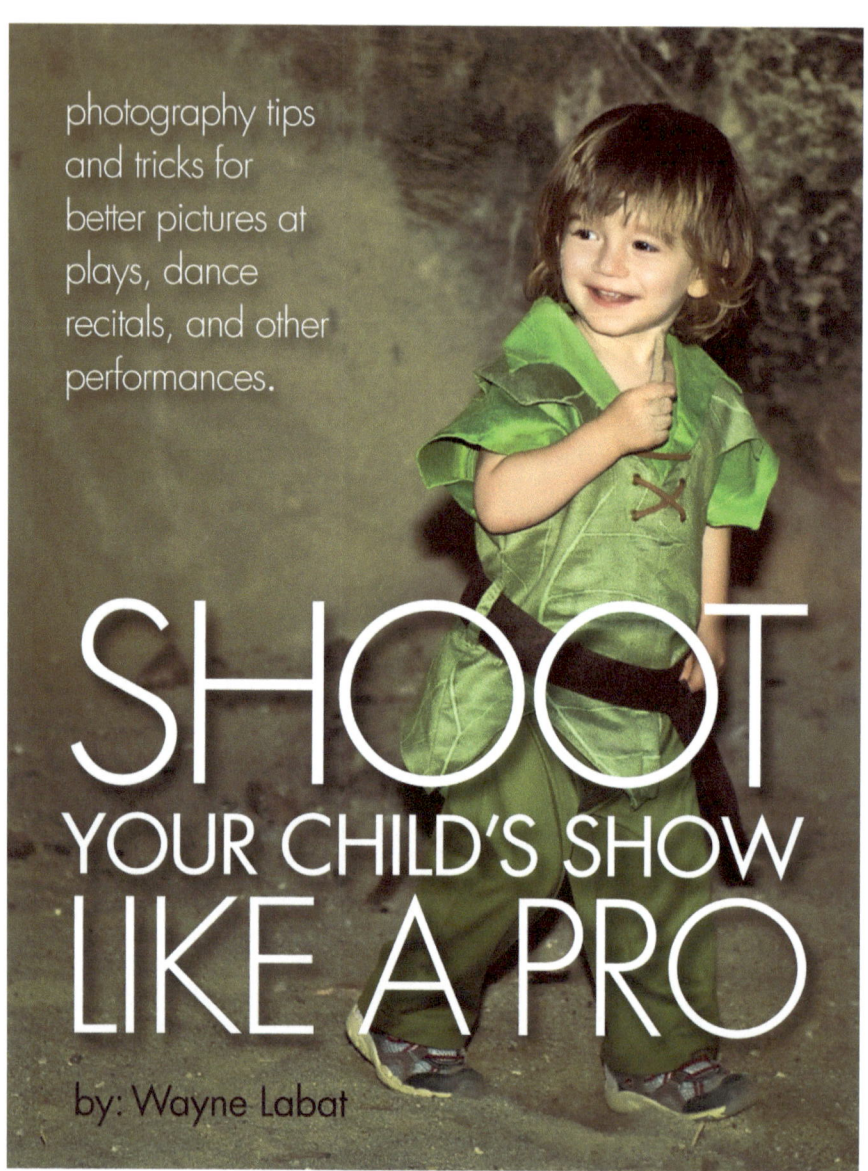

photography tips
and tricks for
better pictures at
plays, dance
recitals, and other
performances.

SHOOT
YOUR CHILD'S SHOW
LIKE A PRO

by: Wayne Labat

www.ingramcontent.com/pod-product-compliance
Lightning Source LLC
Chambersburg PA
CBHW040821180526
45159CB00001B/13